Get Started in
Sage 50

Mac Bride

For UK order enquiries: please contact Bookpoint Ltd,
130 Milton Park, Abingdon, Oxon OX14 4SB.
Telephone: +44 (0) 1235 827720. Fax: +44 (0) 1235 400454.
Lines are open 09.00–17.00, Monday to Saturday, with a 24-hour
message answering service. Details about our titles and how to
order are available at www.teachyourself.com

Long renowned as the authoritative source for self-guided learning –
with more than 50 million copies sold worldwide – the Teach Yourself
series includes over 500 titles in the fields of languages, crafts,
hobbies, business, computing and education.

British Library Cataloguing in Publication Data: a catalogue record
for this title is available from the British Library.

First published in UK 2006 by Hodder Education, part of Hachette
UK, 338 Euston Road, London NW1 3BH.

This edition published 2010.

Previously published as *Teach Yourself* Sage Line 50

The **Teach Yourself** name is a registered trade mark of
Hodder Headline.

Copyright © Mac Bride 2010

Typeset by MPS Limited, a Macmillan company.

Printed in Great Britain for Hodder Education, an Hachette UK
Company, 338 Euston Road, London NW1 3BH, by CPI Cox &
Wyman, Reading, Berkshire RG1 8EX.

The publisher has used its best endeavours to ensure that the URLs
for external websites referred to in this book are correct and active
at the time of going to press. However, the publisher and the
author have no responsibility for the websites and can make no
guarantee that a site will remain live or that the content will remain
relevant, decent or appropriate.

Hachette UK's policy is to use papers that are natural, renewable
and recyclable products and made from wood grown in sustainable
forests. The logging and manufacturing processes are expected to
conform to the environmental regulations of the country of origin.

Impression number   10 9 8 7 6 5 4 3 2 1
Year   2014 2013 2012 2011 2010

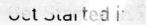
Get Started i

Contents

Welcome to Teach Yourself Sage 50

Sage is the UK's leading accountancy software house, and its central product, Sage 50 Accounts, is the UK's most widely-used accounts system – or rather set of systems. It comes in three sizes: Accounts, Accounts Plus and Accounts Professional. All share a common core, but the latter two have extra features that larger businesses may need – and you can move your data from one to the next as your business grows. (And if it gets really big, there are 200, 500 and 1000 versions, and a whole range of management and analysis software to help you handle other aspects of your business.)

The software follows the standard double-entry, three-ledger approach to bookkeeping, but with the addition of a large set of analysis, reporting and other management information tools, plus the normal time- and effort-saving facilities that you would expect from any good computerized system. This combination of simplicity and comprehensive coverage, plus the tried and tested reliability of the software, are why Sage systems are so widely used.

Chapter 1 provides a brief introduction to the accountancy principles behind the software – because if you understand how a system works and why things are done the way they are, you will master it more quickly and be more able to sort out problems later. The rest of the book demonstrates how to use the various modules and facilities, for day-to-day accounting, for the end-of-period summaries and reports, and for analysis at any time. I have not tried to cover every aspect of the software – there's a comprehensive Help system for that – but instead have concentrated on the essentials, in the hope that this will help to build a firm foundation of understanding and the confidence to tackle the minor features, if you need to use them.

Mac Bride
Southampton, 2010

5 Only got five minutes?

An organization's accounts are the records of its transactions, of the money that comes in and goes out, of what it owes and is owed, of the goods and services that it has bought, holds in stock and has sold, and of the property and equipment that it owns. These transactions must be recorded correctly and promptly, not just so that the taxman can take his fair bite – though that is a factor – but mainly because you need the information at your fingertips to be able to run a business efficiently.

The Sage 50 Accounts window is designed for simple record handling. Once you are comfortable with this window and its tools, you are well on the way to mastering the system.

Let's start at the bottom left and work up and across from there.

The **navigation bar** occupies the left of the window. At the bottom are buttons labelled **Customers**, **Suppliers**, **Company**, **Bank** and **Products**. Sage 50 groups records, and the operations that are performed on them, into modules. These buttons are used to navigate between the modules.

Above these are the **Links list** and the **Tasks list** which lead to jobs related to the current module. Some of these will produce lists in the display area, others will open dialog boxes or new windows for data entry or analysis.

At the heart is the **display area** where the records of the current module are listed. They can be selected here either singly or in groups, to examine them or to enter transactions. Data entry and display of the details of transactions are normally done in separate windows. The buttons at the bottom of the display area can simplify record-handling.

When you switch to a different module, its record display overlays the existing one, but the old one is still there. Look beneath the display area and you will see **tabs**. Click on a tab to bring its module back to the front.

The **tools** above the display area vary according to the module, and the current contents of the display area. Sometimes there will be more tools that can fit across the window, and the extra ones are reached by clicking a marker at the end of the toolbar.

Above the toolbar is the **menu bar** which contains additional commands, mainly concerned with setting up and maintenance, rather than day-to-day operations.

Because a business's accounts are vital to its survival, Sage 50 comes supplied with a set of Demonstration accounts, and has a practice facility. These allow you to explore the system and try out routines before you start to use Sage 50 in earnest. Use these before you start to do anything with your own data, and come back to them whenever you have to do an operation that you are not clear about. You can switch back into either the demo or practice mode at any time without affecting your company data files.

1

The principles of accounts

In this chapter you will learn:
- *why businesses need to keep accounts*
- *about double-entry bookkeeping and the three-ledger system*
- *about the trial balance, profit and loss account and balance sheet*

1.1 The common basis

Though businesses vary enormously in what they do and how they do it, large parts of their accounting systems are essentially the same. An electrician, a violin-maker, a web design partnership, a clothes manufacturer, a chain store and the chap who runs the corner-shop may not seem to have much in common. They deal in different products and services; some employ many people, others work alone; some have many over-the-counter customers, some work for a few carefully-cultivated clients; some deal almost entirely in cash, others trade on credit with their customers and suppliers. Despite this, the basic structures and operations of their accounts are the same.

Every business has:

▶ *Customers, to whom they supply goods or services.*
▶ *Suppliers of goods and services – from accountancy to Yellow Pages ads. A manufacturing business will also have suppliers of raw materials.*

- ▶ *Owner(s) – a sole trader, a group of partners or the shareholders of a company.*
- ▶ *Assets – premises, vehicles, machinery, office furniture and equipment.*

The business may also have **employees**. The standard Sage 50 accounts software handles wages, tax and National Insurance as business expenses, but does not cover employees' individual work records and wage slips. If you are interested, Sage produce Payroll software that is compatible with Sage 50.

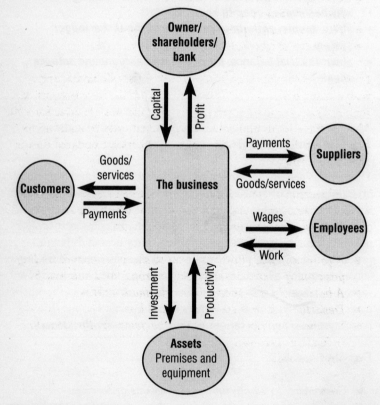

The common structure ... *and the flow of money, goods and services between the components. (Taxes have been omitted for the sake of clarity.)*

1.2 Accounts and information

The purpose of any accounting system is to record transactions and to provide information about the business. It must be able to tell you such things as:

▶ *The amounts you owe to suppliers.*
▶ *The amounts owed to you by customers.*
▶ *The total sales and purchases during a period.*
▶ *The expenses incurred in running the business, e.g. rent, power, stationery, salaries.*
▶ *The value of cash in hand and at the bank.*
▶ *The value of the business's capital assets.*

Most of these amounts and values have to be calculated, and with a manual system, that takes time. With the Sage systems, as with all good accounts software, the calculations are done for you. Most of these totals and values are automatically brought up to date as each new transaction is posted; others are updated during end-of-year routines.

The software can also produce, at a click of a button, a range of financial statements and summaries – all of which can be useful and some of which are essential. These include:

▶ *A profit and loss (P&L) account to show the overall trading position. Is the business making a profit? And how much?*
▶ *A balance sheet showing the assets and liabilities.*
▶ *Departmental analyses of profit and loss.*
▶ *Summaries and graphs showing the patterns of trade with individual customers and suppliers.*
▶ *VAT returns.*

1.3 Double-entry bookkeeping

Double-entry bookkeeping is the basis of all modern accounting systems. It works like this.

A separate *account* – a record of transactions – is kept for each customer and supplier, for each category of expenses, assets and debts, for each bank account, etc.

It is called double-entry bookkeeping because every transaction is recorded twice – as a *debit* in one account and as a *credit* in another. When an item is purchased, its value is added to the appropriate expense or stock account, and the same amount removed from a cash, bank or supplier's account.

Bank Account			
Debit	**£**	**Credit**	**£**
		Purchases	690

Purchases Account			
Debit	**£**	**Credit**	**£**
300 widgets (bank)	690		

▶ A **debit** *is the movement of value into an account – e.g. when goods are purchased, this is a debit in the stock account.*
▶ A **credit** *is the movement of value out of an account, e.g. the money to pay for purchases will come from the bank or cash account, and be recorded as a credit there.*

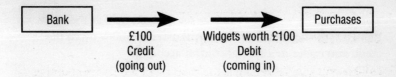

Bank → £100 Credit (going out) → Widgets worth £100 Debit (coming in) → Purchases

Because the movement of money into one account is always balanced by an outward movement from another, the totals of the credits and debits should always be the same. A Trial Balance (page 12), which compares those totals, provides a first-level check of the accuracy of the accounts.

Credit = out debit = in

Newcomers to accounts can sometimes be confused over debit and credit – when you are working with some accounts the use of 'credit' or 'debit' to describe a transaction seems a bit counter-intuitive. The 'real world' use of the terms is much slacker than their use in accounting. Stick to the golden rule: it's a credit when the value is being moved out of the account, and a debit to the account that the value is being moved into.

ASSETS AND LIABILITIES

An **asset** is something which can be turned into cash, so either something that we own, or money that is owed to us. Assets are divided into two categories:

▶ Fixed assets: *those which have more or less constant value, such as buildings, equipment, furnishings and vehicles.*
▶ Current assets: *those which fluctuate during the course of the year as the business trades, such as stock, cash in the bank and monies owed by customers.*

When assets are acquired they are recorded as debit entries in their accounts, with balancing credit entries elsewhere. With purchases of stock and fixed assets, the credit entries will probably be in the bank account. (This 'Bank Account' is your record of cheques paid and received. It is not the same as the account held at the bank, though they should tally.) Where the asset is money owed the credit entry goes in a special control account.

Liabilities are the amounts owed by the business. They are also divided into two categories:

▶ **Capital:** *money invested by the owners (either personally or as shareholders), profits ploughed back into the firm, bank loans and other long-term debts. These may appear in the accounts under the heading 'Financed By'.*
▶ **Current liabilities:** *debts which change during trading – money owed in taxes or to suppliers, bank overdrafts.*

Capital

The term is used loosely to mean several slightly different things. When a business is first started, 'capital' refers to the money put into it to get things going. A loan is sometimes referred to as 'working capital', though strictly speaking this means the difference between current assets and current liabilities. In an ongoing business, capital can be defined as the excess of assets over liabilities – the value of the business if all its assets are sold and debts paid.

EXAMPLE: THE START-UP

Smith and Jones pool their savings to start a business. They begin by buying a machine to make widgets and a van to deliver them. Here are the key accounts after the initial setting up. These are hugely simplified! Transactions would normally be recorded in far more detail – at the very least they should have the date and an invoice or other reference number. There should a clear 'audit trail' – a simple way to trace the flow of money through the business.

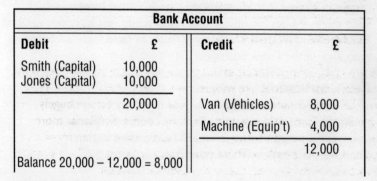

Capital Account

Debit	£	Credit	£
		Smith (Bank)	10,000
		Jones (Bank)	10,000
		Balance	20,000

Vehicles Account

Debit	£	Credit	£
Van (Bank)	8,000		
Balance	8,000		

Equipment Account

Debit	£	Credit	£
Machine (Bank)	4,000		
Balance	4,000		

Bank Account

Debit	£	Credit	£
Smith (Capital)	10,000		
Jones (Capital)	10,000		
	20,000	Van (Vehicles)	8,000
		Machine (Equip't)	4,000
			12,000
Balance 20,000 − 12,000 = 8,000			

Each account has been totalled to give its current balance. As the Bank account has both debit and credit entries, both sides have been totalled and the balance is the difference between the two. Add up debit and credit balances and you get the same £20,000 total.

1.4 Customers and Suppliers

In a paper-based system, the individual accounts are held in *books of account*, or *ledgers* – the *Sales*, *Purchase* and *Nominal ledgers*. The Sage system follows this convention, but refers to the Sales ledger as the *Customers* navigation group or module, the Purchase ledger as the *Suppliers* module and the Nominal Ledger is in the *Company* module.

THE SALES LEDGER (CUSTOMERS)

If customers buy from you on credit, they will each have their own separate account, where you record the date and value of each sale and of each payment made. With Sage software, not only can you easily see which payments are outstanding – and for how long – you can just as easily generate reminder letters to the slower-paying debtors. There are also a report generator, a graph facility and other tools to enable you to analyse and understand the patterns and trends of your trading with any one or more selected customers.

The Sales ledger is a collection of customers' accounts. There will be one or more other accounts – in the Nominal ledger – which keep track of sales overall. A small firm might just have one general Sales account; a larger one is more likely to have Sales accounts for each area of the firm's business.

Cash, not credit

Over-the-counter cash sales would normally be recorded directly into the Sales (and Bank) accounts. Similarly, anything bought for cash would be recorded in the appropriate expenses and purchases accounts.

If you do have purely cash dealings with any customer or suppliers, it may be worth setting up individual accounts for them if you want to monitor your trade with them. One of the reasons for keeping accounts is to collect information which you can use to improve your business. Understanding your trading patterns always helps.

THE PURCHASE LEDGER (SUPPLIERS)

This is the mirror image of the Sales ledger, recording the details of your dealings – on credit – with your suppliers. Each entry will be matched by a balancing entry in the Nominal ledger, where there will be accounts for purchases of stock and raw materials, and other expenses. (NB: in accountancy, *purchases* refers only to raw materials and goods bought for resale; all other costs are *expenses*.)

1.5 The Nominal ledger

This is the heart of a manual system – if you had no credit sales or purchases, it is the only one you would need. All accounts, except those for credit customers and suppliers, are stored here.

The Nominal ledger in Sage 50

In the Sage system, the Nominal ledger accounts are accessed through two modules or navigation groups. The bank and cash accounts, and their associated activities are in the Bank group. The whole ledger, including the bank accounts, with the tools for analysing the finances, and handling end-of-period routines, VAT returns, etc. are in the Company group.

Exactly how you organize your nominal accounts is up to you – they should reflect the realities of your business. As a general rule, you set up an account for each aspect of the money flow that you want to be able to monitor. For example, in a small business, where the office expenses only add up to a few hundred a year, one account would be adequate to record them all. In a larger firm, separate accounts for paper, postage, cleaning, electricity, coffee, etc. would enable managers to see clearly how and when money was being spent – and therefore to forecast future spending, and perhaps find some savings.

Some accounts are essential. You must have ones for:

▶ *Capital and long-term loans*
▶ *Fixed assets*
▶ *Cash in hand and at the bank*
▶ *Sales of goods and services*
▶ *Expenses.*

Retailing or manufacturing businesses also need accounts for:

▶ *Purchases of goods and materials, and current stock*
▶ *Labour, advertising and other expenses directly related to producing and selling goods.*

NOMINAL CODES

The Sage system comes with a comprehensive set of Nominal accounts. We will look later (page 91) at how to adapt or add to these to suit your business; for the moment just notice the way they are organized.

Each account has a reference number, or *nominal code*, with the numbering set so that related ones are close together. When summaries are being prepared, groups of accounts can be totalled simply by setting ranges. For example, the first four are:

0010	Freehold Property
0011	Leasehold Property
0012	Land
0020	Plant and Machinery

The total of the range 0010 to 0012 is the value of all property and land. If you wanted to create accounts for more categories of property or land, by numbering them 0013, 0014, etc., you only need to extend the range to get a summary property value.

A little further down the list you will find

0030	Office Equipment
0040	Furniture and Fixtures
0050	Motor Vehicles

Setting the range 0010 to 0050 will therefore give the value of all fixed assets.

This pattern runs right through the system, with groups of accounts separated from the next by breaks in the number sequence.

THE NOMINAL STRUCTURE

Fixed assets	4900 – Other income
0 – Premises, etc.	**Purchases**
Current Assets	5000 – Materials
1000 – Stock	5200 – Stock
1100 – Debtors	**Direct Expenses**
1200 – Bank	6000 – Labour
Current Liabilities	6200 – Advertising
2100 – Creditors	**Overheads**
2200 – Tax Control	7000 – Wages & Salaries
2300 – Loans	7100 – Premises' costs
Capital & Reserves	7200 – Expenses
3000 – Share capital	8000 – Depreciation
3200 – Profit & Loss	**Trouble-shooting**
Income	9998 – Suspense A/c
4000 – Work done	9999 – Mispostings
4200 – Sales of assets	

An outline of the Nominal ledger structure in Sage 50.

1.6 Analysis and outputs

The accounts themselves are simply records of transactions, but the accounting system is more than that. It is also a means of assessing the health of the business and analysing its performance. There are three key outputs from any manual system, and they are all present – along with many others – in Sage 50. And, of course, the big difference between a manual system and Sage is that with Sage you get the outputs at the touch of a button, instead of having to spend hours, or even days, with a pencil, paper and calculator. The key outputs are the trial balance, the profit and loss account and the balance sheet.

THE TRIAL BALANCE

The trial balance shows the current debit and credit balance on each account, and the total of all debits and credits.

In a manual accounting system, it is used to check that data has been double-entered correctly – the sum of the debit and credit balances should be equal. If they are not, it shows that with at least one transaction, one or both of the values has been entered wrongly or in the wrong column, or has been omitted altogether.

In a Sage system this cannot happen as the value entered for a transaction is automatically posted to two accounts – once as a debit and once as a credit. However, the trial balance is still useful as it gives a convenient summary of the trading figures. If the credit and debit totals didn't balance it would show that the data had become corrupted.

	Bridge Computers Period Trial Balance		
N/C	Name	Debit £	Credit £
0020	Plant and Machinery	18,000.00	
0030	Office Equipment	5,400.00	
0040	Furniture and Fixtures	1,240.00	
0050	Motor Vehicles	11,410.00	
1001	Stock	11,800.00	
1100	Debtors Control Account	7,743.27	
1200	Bank Current Account	1,623.30	

1230	Petty Cash	1,200.00	
2100	Creditors Control Account		10,879.75
2200	Sales Tax Control Account		1,153.27
2201	Purchase Tax Control Account	1,068.45	
3001	Owners' Investment		20,000.00
4000	Computer systems		45,680.00
4001	Peripherals and parts		56,960.00
4002	Software packages		49,197.00
5000	Materials Purchased	62,320.00	
6201	Advertising	1,500.00	
7001	Directors' Salaries	24,000.00	
7004	Wages	29,950.00	
7100	Rent	2,105.00	
7103	General Rates	1,010.00	
7200	Electricity	2,000.00	
7502	Telephone	1,500.00	
	Totals:	183,870.02	183,870.02

PROFIT AND LOSS ACCOUNT

One of the main uses of the information in your accounts is to assess the profitability of your business – and to find ways to make it more profitable. The Profit and Loss account is a key tool for this. It shows the totals of those accounts that are most directly related to trading, and from these it calculates the current stock levels and the gross and net profit.

▶ **Stock:** *purchases plus the difference between the opening and closing stocks.*
▶ **Gross Profit:** *the difference between your sales income and the cost of goods or raw materials plus the labour and other expenses directly incurred in making and selling the goods.*
▶ **Net Profit:** *Gross Profit minus office costs and other general overheads.*

Bridge Computers	
Profit & Loss	
	£
Sales	151,837.00
Purchases	62,320.00
Direct Expenses	
Sales Promotion	1,500.00
Gross Profit/(Loss):	88,017.00
Overheads	
Gross Wages	53,950.00
Rent and Rates	3,115.00
Heat, Light and Power	2,000.00
Printing and Stationery	1,500.00
	60,565.00
Net Profit/(Loss):	27,452.00

A simplified profit & loss account. This is based on the same figures as the trial balance. In sage 50, the Profit & Loss report will normally show two sets of figures – one for the selected period, and one for the year to date.

END OF PERIOD ADJUSTMENTS

Even if you are scrupulous in entering all sales and costs as they occur, your end of period accounts may not give a true picture of the business. Some accounts must be adjusted to reflect the reality of the situation. Stock valuation and depreciation must obviously be handled, and when does a debt become a bad debt?

Another problem is that the expenses entered into the accounts may not relate to the period in question. A business may well pay in arrears for some things and in advance for others. In accounting these are called **accruals** and **prepayments**.

Accruals are monies owing for expenses. Rent, rates, power and phone bills are typically paid in arrears. Even if they are paid on receipt, they are unlikely to coincide exactly with the business's year end. The double-entry solution is to set up an *Accruals* account, and to credit end-of-year bills to this, debiting the matching expense. The true total amount of the expense can then be carried into the Profit and Loss account.

A similar *Prepayments* account can be used in the same way, with debits and credits reversed, to handle prepaid bills.

Telephone Account				
Debit	**£**	**Credit**		**£**
Bank	400			
Bank	450			
Bank	450			
Accruals (31/12)	420			
	1720			

Accruals Account			
Debit	**£**	**Credit**	**£**
		Telephone (31/12)	420

Here the last quarter phone bill was not paid in the financial year, but the cost is taken into the Profit and Loss calculations through the Accruals account.

Accruals and prepayments in Sage 50

Sage 50 has an Accruals account (Nominal Code 2109) and a Prepayments account (Nominal Code 1103). At the end of the year, any outstanding and pre-paid bills should be posted to these through Journal entries (see page 98).

THE BALANCE SHEET

The balance sheet provides a summary of the assets and liabilities of a business — and the two totals must balance, or there is something wrong with the calculations!

Fixed assets are items which have been bought to be retained within the business (for at least a year), and not for resale at a profit. They include equipment, vehicles, property and the like. Any depreciation – or appreciation in value – is entered into the accounts at the end of the period so that a realistic value is present in the balance sheet.

Bridge Computers
Balance Sheet

Fixed Assets	£	£
Plant and Machinery	18,000.00	
Office Equipment	5,400.00	
Furniture and Fixtures	1,240.00	
Motor Vehicles	11,410.00	
		36,050.00
Current Assets		
Stock	11,800.00	
Debtors	7,743.27	
Deposits and Cash	1,200.00	
Bank Account	1,623.30	
		22,366.57
Current Liabilities		
Creditors: Short-term	10,879.75	
VAT Liability	84.82	
		10,964.57
Current Assets less Current Liabilities		11,402.00 #1
Long-term Liabilities	0.00	
Total Assets less Total Liabilities:		47,452.00
Capital & Reserves		
Share Capital	20,000.00	
P&L Account	27,452.00	
		47,452.00

A balance sheet based on the same figures as the earlier trial balance and profit and loss account.

Current assets are those which should be realized (turned into cash) during the year's trading. They are listed in the balance sheet in order of liquidity, with the least liquid at the top.

Current liabilities are the short-term debts owed by the business – principally, the bank overdraft, suppliers' bills not yet paid, and any wages that are due at that point.

Long-term liabilities are loans, mortgages and other debts that will be paid off in instalments over time.

Capital and **Reserves** include share capital and investment by the owner(s). The profit also sits here until it is distributed to the owners or shareholders, or reinvested in the business.

LIQUIDITY

The Current Assets less Current Liabilities figure gives an instant check on the liquidity of the business.

There are two crucial measures that can be drawn from the current assets and liabilities figures.

The **Liquidity Ratio** is a measure of how well a business can find the cash it needs to meet its short-term debts. It is calculated by the simple formula:

$$\text{Liquidity Ratio} = \frac{\text{Current Assets}}{\text{Current Liabilities}}$$

If the ratio is less than 1.0, the business is in trouble. In the Sage Balance Sheet display, the **Current Assets less Liabilities** figure gives a similar guide – this should be a positive value.

In practice, the **Quick Assets Ratio** is a better guide to the ability of a business to survive a crisis. This uses only the most liquid assets and short-term liabilities – those things that can be turned into cash in a hurry:

$$\frac{\text{Cash + Debetors + Cashable Deposits}}{\text{Short + Term Current Liabilities}}$$

THINGS TO REMEMBER

▶ *Businesses of all sizes and types share a common basis and this is reflected in the structure of the accounts.*

▶ *The purpose of accounts is to track the flow of money through the business, to help its managers run it more efficiently, and to provide legally required information to the taxman, VAT man and, where appropriate, Companies House.*

▶ *Double-entry bookkeeping is based on the concept that every transaction is recorded twice – showing where the money went and where it came from.*

▶ *Where sales and purchases are made on credit, transactions with customers are recorded in the Sales Ledger, those with suppliers in the Purchase Ledger.*

▶ *The Nominal Ledger is the heart of the bookkeeping system. It should contain separate accounts to record each type of income and expenditure.*

▶ *In a manual system the trial balance acts as an important check on the accuracy of entries. In Sage systems, it is a useful source of summary information.*

▶ *The Profit and Loss account shows the performance of the business.*

▶ *The Balance Sheet provides a summary of the total assets and liabilities of the business, and shows its current value.*

The Sage 50 system

In this chapter you will learn:
- *about the Sage 50 screen*
- *how to enter and edit data*
- *how to create and edit reports*
- *about file maintenance and backups*
- *about wizards and smart links*

2.1 Getting started

If Sage 50 is already installed in your computer and you have
a user name and password, then skip on to section 2.2. If not,
install the software now – just put the CD in the drive and
follow the instructions. That's all straightforward. The next
stage is a little less obvious. Until you have set it up with
your company data, when you start Sage it will offer you
three choices:

- ▶ *Set up your company data*
- ▶ *Open practice data*
- ▶ *Open demonstration data.*

Welcome to Sage 50 Accounts

Choose one of the following options:

○ **Set up your Company Data**
Start using your own company's data.

◉ **Open Practice Data**
Practice using the program's features without affecting your company's data. This will start as a blank set of company information.

○ **Open Demonstration Data**
See an example company we have created for you. This includes customer and supplier invoices and payments.

OK   Cancel

It's worth exploring the system using the demonstration data, and a good idea to take a test run through the key routines using the practice data mode, but before you can do any of this, you have to log on.

LOG ON

The first time that you use Sage 50, you can only log on with the name 'manager'. There is no password. If you are the only person who will be using the system, and your PC is secure, you could simply leave it this way. But your company data is precious – you should at least add a password. If several people will be working on the accounts, each of them will need a user name. You may as well do this now. Start Sage, select the demonstration data and log on as 'manager'.

Logon

Welcome to Sage 50 Accounts.

Please enter your logon name and password.

Logon   manager

Password

OK

Cancel

Help

To create a user name:

1 *Open the* Settings *menu and select* Access Rights.

2 *You will be warned that you cannot run this with other windows open and that any unsaved data will be lost. This may be worth knowing for future reference, but at this point – just started and with no unsaved data – it is irrelevant.*

3 *At the* User Access Rights *dialog box, click* New.

4 *Enter the user's name and a password. The password should be a bit less guessable than 'LETMEIN' if you want to keep your data secure.*

Create New User

User Details

Logon Name   mac

Password   LETMEIN|

Access Rights

⊙ Full Access   ○ No Access

[Discard]   [Save]   [Close]

5 *Select* **Full Access** *then click* **Save.**
6 *You can repeat steps 4 and 5 to add other user if required –
or come back and add them at another time.*

This gives the user access to all areas of the accounts. If required,
you can set limits on a user's access rights – see section 3.3.

Register and activate

The software is fully functional immediately after installation,
but it will cease to be so after a fairly short period if you
do not register with Sage and activate it. This will only
take a few moments whether you do it online or through
their telephone helpline. You will find the serial number
and activation key in the software's box, on a sheet marked
'Important Information'.

2.2 The screen display

For anyone who has used Windows – and that must be almost
everyone – much of the screen display and the way you interact
with it will be immediately obvious. However, the system does
have a few little wrinkles all of its own.

Tasks list

Links list

Tools

Display area

Navigation group buttons...

... and icons

Control handle

Record-handling buttons

Tabs to switch between open displays

Let's start by looking round the main window.

▶ The **display area** *occupies the most space. It is mainly used for listing and selecting records. Data entry and display of the details of transactions are normally done in dialog boxes or in separate windows.*

▶ The **tools** *above the display area vary to suit the contents.*

▶ **Buttons** *for common record management jobs will be present in the display area if it contains a list.*

- If several lists are open at the same time, each will be identified by a tab at the bottom of the display area. Click on a tab to bring its list to the front.
- The **navigation bar** occupies the left of the window.
- The **Customers, Suppliers, Company, Bank** and **Products** buttons are used to navigate between the groups of operations. They can be shown in full, with text labels, or as icons only on the bar beneath.
- The **Tasks list** shows the tasks that are directly related to the current navigation group. Some of these will produce lists in the display area, others will open dialog boxes or new windows for data entry or analysis.
- The **Links list** leads to operations that are in both the current and in other navigation groups. (The distinction between tasks and links eludes me!)

You can adjust the width of the navigation bar and the depth of each of its sections.

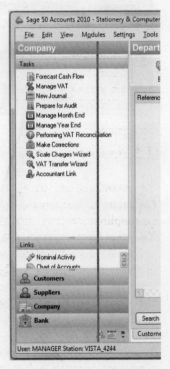

To adjust the width:
1 *Move the pointer over the dividing line until it changes to a double-headed arrow.*
2 *Click on the line, hold down the mouse button and drag the guideline in or out.*
3 *Release the mouse button.*

To change the depth of a section:

1 *Click on the handle at the top of the section.*

2 *Drag it up or down as required. If you shrink the lower section, the buttons will be replaced by icons on the bar beneath.*

Practise first!

Play with Sage 50 before you start to use it in earnest. Start by opening the Practice data, or if you have started in another mode, switch to it with File > Open > Practice Data (i.e. open the File menu, point to Open then select Practice Data). Explore and experiment with these to get the hang of the system. When you are confident that you have understood the principles and the main routines, set to work in earnest.

Later, whenever you are faced with a new operation and are not sure how it works, use the practice data or the demo data again and try things out there.

2.3 Viewing records and transactions

The records of any active account will contain a number of transactions over a period of time, but the account can normally be simplified down to a single figure to express its current status. The records of transactions, such as invoices, may similarly have several levels of complexity – there may be a number of items in an invoice, they may not all be paid for at once, some may be returned, etc. Sometimes you want the simple summary, other times you want to get deeper into the record. Opening up deeper levels of details is known as 'drilling down'.

As a general rule, if you have a list of records or transactions on screen and want to look at one in more detail, double-clicking on it will display it in the next level of detail. This does not always work, and sometimes there are alternatives, but both these situations are easily recognized.

- *In the Customers, Suppliers and similar lists, you will see a Record button in the toolbar. Click this to open a window to display the currently selected record. (If several records are selected, it will initially display the topmost. Click **Next** to bring the next record into view.)*

- *In the displays of invoices and similar records of transactions, you will see an arrow icon ◯ beside items. Click on this to display the details of the item. You can often add notes here, and change the details if the transaction has not yet been taken into the system.*

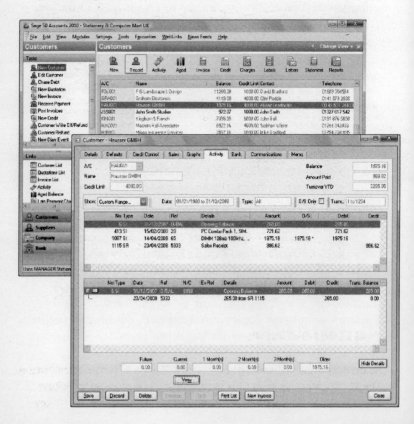

Displaying the details of a transaction.

ALTERNATIVE VIEWS

At the top right of some displays you will see a Change View button. The Customers, Suppliers, Company and Products modules have a Dashboard view, which shows graphs or text summaries of key aspects of the accounts. Customers and Suppliers also have a Process view which offers an alternative way to the Tasks for starting jobs.

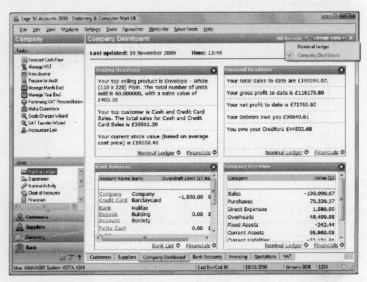

The Dashboard view in the Company module.

2.4 Entering data

For the most part, you use the standard Windows techniques – i.e. type in your text, using backspace to rub out errors, and the arrow keys to move around within text. However, there are also a few special techniques that you should learn.

TEXT ITEMS

You very rarely write continuous text when doing the accounts. Almost all text will be short items – names, addresses and other details of new customers, entries on invoices, and the like. Each of these items will normally go into a separate field (text box) on screen.

▶ *If you have something that you want to spread over several lines, such as the details in a service invoice, press* [Enter] *at the end of each line.*

- ▶ *When you want to go to the next field, press* [**Tab**].
- ▶ *If you need to go back to a field to correct an entry, hold* [**Shift**] *and press* [**Tab**].

Click to bring tab to the front

Number entry

Drop-down list

Phone dialler

A typical data entry/display window. Most of these are tabbed windows – click on the label to bring its tab to the front.

EASY DATA ENTRY

Sage 50 provides easy ways to enter numbers, dates and any information that is already in your files.

Numbers

When you go to a number field, you will usually see a calculator icon by the side. Click on this and a small calculator will appear. Click on the digits to enter a number or use it as a calculator to work out discounts or other values. Click the '=' button to show the result and exit.

Backspace   Clear entry

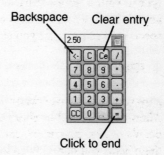

Click to end

Dates

The Program Date (normally the current date, but see page 78) is entered automatically into date fields. If you want to change it, click the mini-calendar icon to open the calendar display. Select the date and press [Esc] or click elsewhere on screen to close the calendar. These dates appear in Day/Month order; elsewhere in the system you'll sometimes find them in Month/Day order.

Previous year
Previous month
Next month
Click to select day

Drop-down lists

When you are creating an invoice and need the details of a customer, then – as long as it is already in the system – the information can be pulled out by selecting from the list that drops down at the side of the field. Accounts, names of suppliers, product details and similar data can likewise be selected from drop-down lists.

2.5 Selections

Before you can edit, delete or in any other way process a record or account, it must be selected. This is done by clicking anywhere on its line in its window.

Multiple selection

In the Customers, Suppliers, Nominal, Products and Invoicing windows, any number of records can be selected at any one time – and once selected, a record stays selected until you deselect it. This is a valuable feature as it allows you to process records in batches.

For example, one of your first jobs when setting up Sage 50 will be to work through the Nominal accounts entering opening balances. If you first go through the list and select all the relevant ones, you can then work steadily through the opening balances routine without having to keep coming back to select the next record.

To select multiple records:

1 *Click on them! (That's it, no need to hold down [Ctrl] as in most Windows applications.)*

2 *If you want all but a few of the records, select the ones you don't want, then click* **Swap** *to invert the selection.*

3 *If you select one by mistake, click on it again to deselect.*

4 *If you have selected several then decide that you do not want them, you can deselect them all by clicking* **Clear**.

Selecting a batch of records for processing.

Single selection

Only one record can be selected at a time in the Bank and Financial modules. Clicking on a record automatically deselects any other selection. Similarly, only one item can be selected in the panels that display the details of records. In most of these cases, 'selecting' a record or item does no more than highlight it for easier identification, as they cannot be edited or processed.

Delete with care!

In the Sage system, when a record has been selected it stays selected – so that multiple selections can be made. Just in case some off-screen records are selected, click **Clear** to deselect all records before selecting any for deletion.

2.6 Wizards

Wizards are routines designed to help you perform operations that might otherwise be tricky. You will meet them when you first set up Sage 50 for your system, whenever you create a new customer, supplier or other account, when you are doing transfers and adjustments within your Nominal Ledger, and in similar situations. At the very least, they help to ensure that you supply the right kind of information and that it goes into the right place.

The examples here are from the Customer Record Wizard, but all wizards work in much the same way. With the information gathering wizards, such as this one, it is best if you have all the necessary information on hand at the start. However, if you don't have it, or don't have time to complete working through the wizard, it won't matter too much, as the record can be edited and new data added at any time.

1   *Start the wizard. Select Customers in the navigation group to display the Customer List and click the* **New** *button or select* **New Customer** *in the* Tasks.
2   *Read the prompts and enter information or select optional settings where indicated.*
3   *Click* **Next** *to go on to the next panel.*
4   *If you want to correct an error, click* **Back** *to return to the panel.*
5   *If you decide to abandon the operation, click* **Cancel**.
6   *If you are not sure what to do at any stage, click* **Help**.
7   *At the last panel, click* **Finish** *to save your information.*

An early stage of the Customer Record Wizard.

The Help page that is displayed by the Help button in the Customer Record Wizard. If text is in green, but turns blue when you point to it, you can click on it to get an explanation of what the term means or what is required of you at that point.

The window warning

This is a minor point, but worth noting as it can throw you the first time you meet it. When you select some routines, you will see a Confirm dialog box, warning you that all open windows must be closed and any unsaved data may be lost. This only refers to windows within the Sage system – if you are also running a browser or word processor or other application at the same time, it will not be affected.

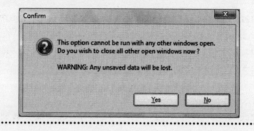

2.7 Smart links

Smart links offer a direct connection to related records. For example, when compiling an invoice, you may need to check or change some details in the customer's record. You could reach that record by going back into the main display, then opening it from the customer list, but there's a quicker way. Next to the customer's account reference, there is button with a fat arrow icon. This is a smart link. Click on it and the customer's record window will open immediately.

Smart link ———

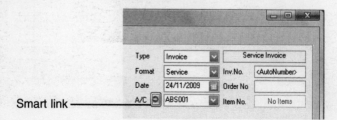

2.8 The Diary

The Diary can be used to record and remind you about meetings and accounting tasks – and birthdays, dental appointments, lunch dates or anything else that you like! It is compatible with the Calendar in Microsoft Outlook, and works in much the same way.

Click the **Diary** button at the bottom of the navigation area to open it. The Diary can be viewed in Day, Work week, Week or Month mode, and as a calendar or as a ToDo list. The view you use affects how you do some jobs.

To create a new event in Day view
1 *If necessary, click the **Day** button on the toolbar to switch to Day view.*
2 *Scroll down and select the time slots when the event will occur. (This is optional – the time can be set at the next stage).*

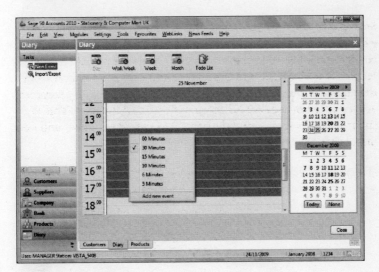

3 *Right-click on the selected times (or anywhere on the day if you have not selected times slots) and select* Add new event *from the pop-up menu.*

4 *At the* **Event** *dialog box, enter the Subject, Location, Contact and other details as relevant.*

5 *If the time slots were not selected, set the times now. Note that you can tick the checkbox to mark this as an All day event.*

6 *If a Reminder is needed, tick the checkbox, set the amount of notice and add a note, if wanted.*

7 *Click* **Save** *to close the dialog box.*

To create a recurring event:

1 *Work through steps 1 to 6 as for a single event.*

2 *Click the* **Recurrence** *button.*

3 Set the **Recurrence pattern**, *then specify the details.*
4 *If this is only to be done a set number of times, or until a certain date, define the* Range of recurrence.
5 *Click* **OK**.

If necessary you can reopen the item later – double-click it, or right-click on it and select **Edit the event**.

If an event is cancelled, or done with and you don't need to keep a record, you can delete it. Right-click on it and select **Delete the event**.

The diary in week view. The todo view simply lists the tasks and their details that need to be done that day, week or month.

2.9 Report Designer

Sage 50 has a wide selection of ready-made letters, statements and other document formats which should be adequate for most accounting purposes. They are standardized, but if they are not quite what you need, you can edit them – you may want to add the Balance to your reminder letters. You can also create your own documents from scratch. The same Report Designer window opens, whether you are working on a label, letter, statement or report.

You can get into the Report Designer in two ways.

The Customers, Suppliers, Company and Bank windows have toolbar buttons for letters, reports or whatever layouts are available in that module. Each button will lead to a dialog box offering you a choice of ready-made report layouts. These can be edited if necessary.

A layout document is made up of elements:

▶ **Text**, *written in separate boxes – the box will expand as you type. The text can be fomartted as in Word.*
▶ **Lines** *and* **boxes**, *for marking off areas.*
▶ **Images**, *such as your company logo, which can either be embedded or linked into the report file. (Use linked for images that may change – the current version will be used when producing the report.)*
▶ **Variables** *which draw data from your files.*
▶ **Expressions** *which perform calculations on the data.*
▶ **Barcodes**, *for use on product labels, etc.*

EDITING A REPORT

There is nothing to stop you creating your own report from
scratch, but it can be a fiddly job getting them to look good.
You will save yourself a lot of time and energy if you can find a
ready-made layout that will do the job, or that needs only a little
adjustment to suit your requirements. Here's how to edit a layout.
In this example, it's a reminder letter, and I want it to include the
amount outstanding.

1   *In the Customer module, select the customers to whom
    reminder letters are to be sent.*
2   *Click the* **Letters** *button.*

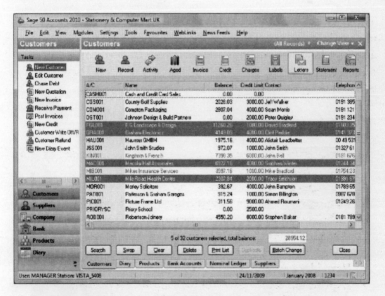

3   *At the Report Browser window, select a report – Payment
    Reminder v.1 in this case – and click the* **Edit** *button.*

4 *The Sage Report Designer window will open – it will take a few moments to get started and load in the report template.*

The Report Designer window, with the reminder letter. Clicking the Toolbox tab, on the left of the window, has brought the Toolbox into view. The variables are labelled in capitals, for easy identification. They can be formatted as ordinary text, and can be spliced into – or on top of – a text box, though perfect alignment is tricky!

ADDING TEXT

Text can be added anywhere on the report, but is written in text boxes.

1   *Open the Toolbox and select the Textbox tool.*
2   *Click onto the report and drag a rectangle approximately where you want the text to appear. It can be moved or resized later.*
3   *Type your text. If there is too much to fit, drag on the bottom or right edge of the box to expand it.*
4   *Click anywhere out of the box to end the text-entry mode.*

To format the text, you must first select it:
1   *To select all text in the box, click once on the box.*
2   *To select some of the text within a box, click once in the box to make it active, then click and drag over the text.*
3   *Use the buttons in the Formatting toolbar to set the font, size, emphasis or alignment.*

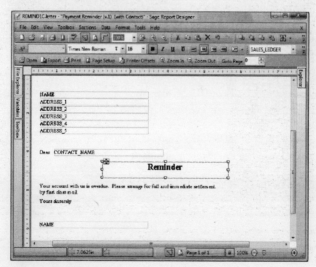

To move a text box, drag on the four-headed arrow. Use the handles on the corners and sides to change its size.

ADDING VARIABLES

1 Click the Variables tab on the left of the frame to display the Variable list.
2 Variables are grouped by category. Click the plus sign to open up a group – it can take a bit of exploring to discover where everything is stored, and what it is called, though much of it is fairly obvious. We're after the outstanding balance, and we can find this in the Sales Ledger group, and it's called BALANCE.
3 Drag the variable onto the report and drop it where you want the data to go. You can adjust its size and location later, if necessary.
4 Use the Formatting toolbar to format the variable as needed. Number variables are right-aligned. You might find it easier to work them into the text of the letter if you change the alignment to left.

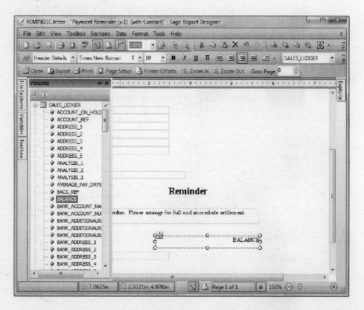

Adding lines and boxes

Lines and boxes are useful for separating areas in a long report, or for making things stand out in a report or letter. Click and drag to draw them on the report, then use the handles to adjust their size and position.

PAGE SETUP

You may want to change the margins, as the defaults are small.

1 *Click the Page Setup button, or open the* **File** *menu and select* **Page Setup.**
2 *In the Margins area, type in new values for the margins. Sage 50 normally uses millimetres. You can change to inches or points in the* **Tools > Options** *dialog box.*
3 *Click* **OK.**

Previewing before you print is always a good idea – especially when you have started from scratch. Things to check:

▶ *Are variable boxes wide enough to fit their data?*
▶ *Do variables line up properly with text in text boxes?*
▶ *Are any labels or headings spelled correctly?*
▶ *Is the spacing between boxes balanced?*

1 *Use* **View > Preview** *to start.*
2 *You can preview the reports for all the selected records, but for the first check, you only need a few samples – set it to two or three.*

The Criteria Values dialog box. The Address Reference feature allows you to specify a range of records in several different ways.

Use the Zoom button to check the layout in detail, if necessary.

Save it!

Don't forget to save your report design when you have finished – you'll need it later. Open the **File** menu and select **Save As**. Give it a name that will identify it clearly.

2.10 File maintenance

All data needs a certain amount of maintenance to be kept in good order. Sage 50 has a set of commands to help maintain your data. One of these should be used as a matter of routine, four will probably be needed from time to time, and there's one that you will hope that you never have to use in earnest!

▶ *Open the* File *menu and select* Maintenance... *to display the* File Maintenance *dialog box.*

All the operations start from here.

Check data

The Check data routine will scan your files, and the links between them, to make sure that your data is in good order. If all is well – and it almost certainly will be – you will get this message:

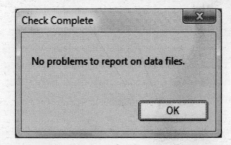

If things have gone awry, the File Maintenance Problems Report window will be displayed. The Summary will give you an overview. To get the details of any errors, warnings or comments, switch to the appropriate tab. There is a Fix facility that should be able to correct the errors, but if this doesn't work it almost certainly means that your files are corrupted and should be restored from the backups (see page 51).

Warnings and comments, if any, will normally relate to minor inconsistencies which you should be able to correct from within the system.

CORRECTIONS

If an error is made when entering a transaction, or a transaction is cancelled after it has been entered into the system, you may be able to delete or edit it through the Corrections routine.

▶ *Bank transfers (page 175) and Journal entries (page 98), which have matching double-entries, cannot be deleted and you can only edit non-critical information, such as Department codes and descriptive text.*

▶ *If you cannot correct the errors here, you can issue credit notes to nullify invoices or make Journal entries to reverse mispostings.*

1 *On the File Maintenance screen, click the **Corrections** button.*
2 *Select the transaction and click the **Edit Item** button in the toolbar.*

3 *If the transaction has not been reconciled on the VAT return, it can be deleted – click **Delete Item** if you want to do this.*
Editing transactions
4 *Edit the information in the Invoice **Details** area as needed.*

Number 1179, Sales Invoice

You can change details of all grouped items at once by using the fields below, or select individual transactions in the list to amend a specific item.

Sales Invoice Details

Account	SPEC01	Due on	31/05/2009
		Last charge	/ /
Reference	70	Int. rate	0.00
Description	Install 4 PCs as requested (PC Con	Posted by	MANAGER
Created on	01/05/2009		
Posted on	30/08/2009	VAT Rec. Date	30/06/2008

Totals

Net	4500.00	Tax	700.00	Paid	0.00

To edit details of a specific item on this Sales Invoice, highlight the item and click 'Edit'. **Edit**

No N/C	Details	Net T/C	Tax
1179 4000	Install 4 PCs as requested (P...	4500.00 T1	700.00

How will this affect my data?   Save   Close

5 *To edit the details of an invoice, select the item and click* **Edit**.

Number 1179, Sales Invoice

Item Details

N/C	4000
Details	Install 4 PCs as requested (PC Combo F
Date	01/05/2008
Department	1
Ex.Ref	

Amounts

Net	4500.00	Tax	787.50	T/C	T1 17.50	Paid	0.00

Flags

Payment Allocations

Type	Date	Payment Ref	Details	Amount

Edit

Close

6 *Edit the* **Details** *and* **Amounts** *as needed and click* **Close.**
7 *Click* **Save** *to write the changes to the files. You will be prompted to confirm that you really want to do this.*
8 *Click* **Close.**

Compression

When transactions, records and other data items are deleted – either through corrections or, more commonly, as part of clearing the audit trail (see page 181) – the data initially remains in the files, but is flagged so that it is ignored by the system. The compression routine works through the files, removing all those records marked as 'deleted'. It is something that should be done from time to time to save disk space and to improve the efficiency of your data-handling.

Always run the Check Data routine first. If there are problems in the files, they should be found and fixed before compression.

1 *Open the* **File** *menu and click* **Maintenance.**
2 *Click* **Compress Data.**

3 *If you only want to compress certain files, clear the* **Compress All Data Files** *checkbox and select the required files.*
4 *Click* **Compress.**
5 *You will be told when compression is complete. Click* **Close** *to exit the routine.*

ReIndex

Indexing allows a data file to be searched more efficiently – and note that the index is only visible to the progam, and not to you. Over time, additions, deletions and alterations to a file make the index less cleanly structured and less efficient to use. There may come a point where reindexing is worth considering. However, this is not to be undertaken lightly, as the process can damage the files! If you know that the files have undergone a lot of changes, and it seems to be taking ever longer to pull up records from the files, contact customer support and discuss reindexing with them before doing anything.

Rebuild

Also not to be used lightly – in fact, not to be used at all in normal circumstances! This routine erases all your data files so that you can start again from scratch. The only time that you would probably want to use this would be after you have been working with the dummy data to get the hang of the system. Rebuild clears away the rubbish ready to start work in earnest.

Recalculate monthly totals

This is another just-in-case function. If your files have been corrupted and you have lost the monthly totals, this routine will recalculate them as far as possible from available data.

2.11 Backups

Once you start to use Sage 50 in earnest, you must get into the habit of backing up your files regularly. The Sage system is very reliable but computers get stolen or damaged, and hard disks can fail. Would your business survive if it lost all its accounts data? More specifically, how much data can you afford to lose and still survive?

A backup file will store that precious accounts data – it will also hold your configuration settings and company details. Backups should be made:

▶ *Daily, or at most weekly, depending upon the number of transactions going through the accounts.*
▶ *On removable media, stored away from the computer, in a fireproof safe, and preferably in another building.*
▶ *With each backup on a separate disk or tape, so that if one is destroyed or corrupted, there is a recent previous version to work from. If you do daily backups, you might have a set of 5 (or 6) that you recycle weekly.*

If you have not backed up recently, you will be prompted when you close down Sage 50. But don't wait for the prompt – get into the habit.

1 *Open the* **File** *menu and select* **Backup...**
2 *On the Backup Company tab, select the drive and directory, and edit the name as required.*
3 *On the Advanced Options tab, tick or clear the checkboxes to select the file types to back up.*
4 *Click* **OK**.

Set the filename and location.

Select which things to backup.

Backup

Progress

Disk: 1

File: CISMONTHLYSTATEMENT.LAY(

Size: 57344 bytes

Total: 1386699 bytes

Cancel

5 *Wait while the files are saved – this could take some time.*

RESTORING FILES

If the worst happens and you have a hard disk crash or lose the
data in any other way, you can recreate the files – if necessary on a
new computer – using the Restore routine.

Restore

Restore Company | Previous Backups

Which backup do you want to restore?

If it is on a floppy disk or other storage media, insert into the drive now.

File: I:\SageAccts Bridge Computers 2009-12-03 17-19-31. ([Browse...]

Description of Data to be restored for: Bridge Computers

Bridge Computers
Backup of :
  - Data Files.
  - Report Templates.
  - Layout Templates.
  - Audit Trail History.
  - Company Archives.

Backup Details

Company Name: Bridge Computers

Data Version: V16

Your backup will be restored to

Company Name: Bridge Computers

Location: C:\PROGRAMDATA\SAGE\ACCOUNTS\2010\COMPANY. 000\

OK | Cancel | Help

You can watch the progress if you are interested – but it's not exciting viewing.

You will lose all the transactions that have been recorded since the backup, but if you have been maintaining the files properly and backing up regularly, they should not take long to re-enter.

1 *Open the* **File** *menu and select* **Restore...**
2 *Click the Browse button and locate the backup file to use.*
3 *Click* **OK.**
4 *Wait while the files are copied back into place. This could take a while so you may as well take a break.*

Which backup?

You normally restore from the most recent backup, though you may have to use an earlier one, if the files had been corrupted – without anyone noticing – at the time of the last backup (which is why you should check the data first).

THINGS TO REMEMBER

▶ *There are some neat tools to simplify data entry. Numbers can be entered (after calculating, if needed) through a mini-calculator; dates through a calendar; and account codes through drop-down lists.*

▶ *Records are selected by clicking on them. In most module windows, any number of records can be selected for processing in a batch.*

▶ *There are wizards to guide you through some of the trickier jobs.*

▶ *Smart links offer a direct connection to related records.*

▶ *You may find the Diary useful for reminding you of jobs that need doing.*

▶ *You can create new reports, or edit existing layouts using Report Designer.*

▶ *The data maintenance routines should keep your data files in good order...*

▶ *...but you must take regular backups, to safeguard against loss of data.*

3

....

Setting up the accounts

In this chapter you will learn:
- *how to configure Sage 50 to suit your business*
- *about the preferences and other default settings*
- *how to change the program date or password*

Practise!

If you are completely new to Sage, and are planning to use it
for your own business's accounts, it really is a good idea to take
a few hours to work through the procedures for setting up the
accounts, and for processing the common transactions using
practice data. Don't go live with your own data until you have a
reasonable grasp of how the system works. You do not need to
understand every detail – much can be learned as and when you
need it – but you do need an overview so that things make sense.

3.1 Company data

Before you start, make sure that you have these things at hand:

▶ *The software's serial number and activation key – you will
find these in the pack. If you have already activated the
program, you won't need these.*

▶ *Your company's contact details, financial year start date, and
VAT registration number. If the company uses the VAT Cash
Accounting scheme, there is an option to set during the setup.
If necessary, check with your accountant or your local VAT
office before running the wizard.*

If you are setting up Sage 50 for the first time, the wizard will create a basic set of nominal ledger accounts. But different types of business need different structures of accounts – a lawyer won't have retail sales or need to record products in stock – so make sure that you pick the type of company which best matches yours when you reach the My Company stage. The set of accounts probably won't be exactly as you want it, but it will form a solid basis which you can later add to or adapt to meet your needs.

1 *At the* **Welcome** *screen select Open Your Company's Data (or Open Practice Data) and click* **OK**.
2 *The Active Setup Wizard will run. At the first stage, select Set up a new company (unless you are importing existing data).*
3 *Enter your* **Company Details** *and click Next.*

4 *At* **Business Type** *pick the type which is closest to yours – the Preview lists the main accounts. General is a good basis for most retail or wholesale businesses.*
5 *At* **Financial Year**, *pick the month when your year starts.*
6 *At* **VAT Details**, *enter your VAT number. Select the option if you use the Cash Accounting scheme.*

ActiveSetup Wizard

Sage Accounts - Company Set-up

1. Welcome
2. Company Details
3. Business Type
4. Financial Year
5. VAT
6. Currency
7. Activate Program
8. Finish

Select Business Type ?

Select a type of business that most closely matches your own. If your business type is not listed, please select General.

Preview

- ⊙ General (standard)
- ○ Accountancy   ○ Hotels
- ○ Agriculture   ○ Legal
- ○ Building   ○ Medical
- ○ Charity   ○ Transport
- ○ Garage   ○ Customised

Sales (Money In)
Sales Type A
Sales Type B
Sales Type C

Costs (Money Out)
Materials Purchased
Materials Imported
Miscellaneous Purchases

Cancel   Back   Next

ActiveSetup Wizard

Sage Accounts - Company Set-up

1. Welcome
2. Company Details
3. Business Type
4. Financial Year
5. VAT
6. Currency
7. Activate Program
8. Finish

Select VAT Details

Is your company VAT registered?

⊙ Yes   ○ No

Enter your VAT registration number   479 815 07   ?

Is your company using the VAT cash accounting scheme? ?

⊙ Yes   ○ No

Enter your standard VAT rate %   15.00   ?

Contact your accountant if you need further guidance

Cancel   Back   Next

---

7 At **Currency**, *select the default currency used for billing.*

8 At **Activate Program** *enter the software's serial number and activation key. If you have any problems with this, the phone line help desk is very good.*

9 *At the final stage, check the details. If you spot an error, use the Back key to return to the relevant stage to correct it, otherwise click Finish.*

ActiveSetup Wizard

Sage Accounts - Company Set-up

1 Welcome
2 Company Details
3 Business Type
4 Financial Year
5 VAT
6 Currency
7 Activate Program
8 Finish

Finished
You have entered the following details, select Back to amend any details or Finish to accept the details and create your company

What you have entered...

Company Name: Bridge Computers

Street 1:   11 The High Street
Street 2:   ——
Town: Oldbridge
County: Midshire
PostCode: OB1 2NB
Country: United Kingdom   GB

Business Type: General(Standard)
Financial Year
Start: May 2009

VAT Registration
Number: 479 815 07
VAT Scheme: VAT cash accounting
Currency: Pound Sterling

Cancel   Back   Next   Finish

3.2 Details and defaults

You will have set up some of the details and defaults for your company during installation. Default settings for customers and suppliers, the organization of the business into departments and of products into categories, may also have been set up then. Any information that was not entered then, or has changed since, can be put in through the Configuration Editor or the Company Preferences options.

THE CONFIGURATION EDITOR

The Configuration Editor dialog box has a dozen tabs. We will be dipping into this from time to time as we cover the parts of the system to which they apply, but there are a couple of tabs that we will have a look at now.

Configuration templates
If you want to have a rethink about which chart of accounts would be best to start from, you can pick a different company type on the General tab.

1 *Open the* **Settings** *menu and select* **Configuration...**

2 *On the* **General** *tab, click Browse to open the* **Company Configurations** *dialog box.*

3 *Scroll through the list and select the most suitable template for your business.*

4 *Click* **Open** *to apply the template.*

Analysing your customers and suppliers

If your company is organized into regions, and/or has several branches, and/or some other form of subdivision, these can be written into the Sage 50 system and used when creating invoices and analysing activity. Even if there are no actual divisions, it can be useful to set up 'virtual' ones for each area of the firm's work, as this will enable you to see more easily the relative profitability of each.

1 *Switch to the* **Custom Fields** *tab.*
2 *Click into the first field under either Customers and replace 'Analysis 1' with a word to describe the sub-division, e.g. 'Region'.*
3 *For a second analysis type, click into the second field and type in the term, e.g. 'Branch'.*
4 *Repeat for a third type if necessary.*
5 *Click* **Apply** *to write the changes into the system.*

Analysis fields for suppliers are set up in exactly the same way.

Departments

Notice the Departments Label at the bottom. Sage assumes that if the firm has subdivisions, these will be called 'departments'. If you use a different term, e.g. 'sectors', you can write that in here. The names for the departments (or sectors...) are entered and edited through the Company module (see Chapter 4).

Fixed Assets

You may find it useful to organize fixed assets into categories, because, as with customers and suppliers, this can improve the quality of the analysis. Spend a little time thinking about this before doing anything, and don't forget that there will be a number of fixed assets accounts in any case. Categories are worth setting up if there are many fixed assets accounts, which could be grouped for more efficient handling in reports.

1 *Switch to the* **Fixed Assets** *tab.*

2 *Select into the first unused field and click* **Edit.**
3 *Type in a name and click* **OK.**

4 *Repeat as necessary – and remember you can add more at any time.*
5 *Click* **Apply,** *then click* **Close.**

COMPANY PREFERENCES

The **Company Preferences** dialog box has eight panels. Two need to be checked and perhaps changed now – the **Address** and the **Parameters** – especially if several people work on the accounts.

To edit and set preferences:

1 *Open the* Settings *menu and select* Company Preferences...
2 *On the* Address *panel, enter your contact details, if these are not already there from the initial setup. These will be used on your letters and invoices.*
3 *The* Labels *panel is probably best left alone until you really know the system. This controls which fields are included in the customer, supplier and product records.*
4 *On the* Parameters *panel, set the options as required. Notice the Access Rights option in the lower set. If more than one person will be keeping the accounts, and you want to set limits to which parts of the accounts they can access and change, turn this on.*

5   The **Reporting** tab sets basic defaults for printed reports and letters and the format for e-mails.

6   The **Accountant** tab holds the contact details of the firm's accountant.

7   **Sage Pay** is a secure service for handling mail order and telephone orders. You can set up an account and enable the service from this tab.

8   On the **VAT** tab, check the settings, and enter your details for online submissions.

9   On the **Budgeting** tab, leave the Method as Standard to have a basic monthly budget against individual nominal accounts, or change to Advanced, and select the Type.

10   When you have worked through the tabs, click **OK**.

3.3 Multiple users and access rights

Where several people work on the accounts, each should be set up as a user on the Sage system – you saw how to do this back in section 2.1. If these people have different responsibilities or different levels of skill, you may need to restrict their access to certain areas and/or to certain tasks within areas. Sage gives you a way to set precise limits to access. The process is – frankly – fiddly, but should only need to be done once for each person – or once for each job specification where several people have the same responsibilities and the same access limits.

1 *Turn on Access Rights in the Company Preferences.*
2 *Open the* **Settings** *menu and select* **Access Rights...**

User Name	Access Type	Password Required
mac	Partial	Yes
joyce	Full	Yes
shu'ab	Full	Yes
ernie	None	No

User Access Rights

New   Edit   Delete   Copy   Details   Close

3 *Select the user and click* **Details.**
4 *You can set access rights to whole modules, or to dialog boxes – the windows in which tasks are carried out.*

To set access at module level:
5 *Click* **Modules.**
6 *Select the module(s), then click* **Full Access** *or* **No Access.**
7 *Click* **OK** *to save the settings.*

To select a lot of options, it is quicker to select the ones you don't want and click Swap to reverse the selection.

To set access at dialog level:

8 *Select the module containing the relevant dialog boxes.*

9 *Click* **Dialogs**.

10 *Select the operations(s), then click* **Full Access** *or* **No Access**.

11 *Save and exit as before.*

CREATING USERS BY COPYING

On the **User Access Rights** dialog box you will see Copy. You can use this to create a new user with the same access rights as an existing one. Now you see why I suggested finishing on the first user before starting the second! Even if the rights are a little different from any other user, starting from a similar level will often be quicker than starting from scratch.

1 *On the* **User Access Rights** *dialog box, select the user with the closest set of access rights.*
2 *Click* **Copy.**

Copy User

Copy details of shu'ab to

Logon Name   Robin

Password

OK   Cancel

3 *Enter the* **Logon Name** *and* **Password** *to create the user and click* **OK.**
4 *Back at the* **User Access Rights** *dialog box, select the copied user and click* **Edit.**
5 *Make any necessary changes at module or dialog level.*

3.4 Customers and suppliers

The Customers and Suppliers defaults follow the same pattern – and some of the settings apply to both. They are controlled through the Configuration Editor, and through the Customer and Supplier Defaults dialog boxes.

1 *Use* Settings > Configuration... *to open the* Configuration Editor, *then work through the tabs as detailed below.*
2 *Click* Apply *and* Close *when you are finished to fix the settings.*

Terms

What is your normal credit limit for a new customer? When is payment due? Do you offer a discount for early settlement? And what do your suppliers normally set as the limits, due dates and discounts?

Change as needed

Remember that these are only the default settings. When you are creating a new customer or supplier account, you can change the settings as needed.

Dispute reasons

If you are in dispute with a customer or supplier, you may find it useful to be able to apply a predefined 'dispute reason' to the account, instead of writing a note. Initially only 'No reason' is defined – you may want to set up a bank of reasons. Whether or not this is worth the time depends upon how often you are likely to be in dispute, so you might want to leave this until later.

To set up dispute reasons:
1 *Switch to the* **Dispute Reasons** *panel.*
2 *Select an unused line and click* **Edit.**

3 *Type the reason and click* **OK.**

4 *Repeat to create your standard set of reasons.*

ACCOUNT STATUS

This is similar to Dispute Reasons in providing a set of labels that can be attached to an account, but will almost certainly be of more use to more people. As well as showing the status of the account, these can also be set to put an account on hold.

There are 10 ready-made status descriptions – mostly relating to problem accounts, and these are all set so that the account is put on hold when the status is applied.

To change or create an account status:
1 *Switch to the* **Account Status** *panel.*
2 *Select the status to change, or an unused line to create a new status.*
3 *Click* **Edit***.*

4 *Type a Description.*
5 *If you want these accounts to be marked 'On Hold', tick the checkbox.*
6 *Click* **OK***.*

CUSTOMER DEFAULTS

1 *Use* **Settings > Customer Defaults…** *to open the* **Customer Defaults** *dialog box, then work through the tabs.*
2 *Click* **OK** *when you are done to fix the settings.*

Records
These defaults are applied to new transactions on customers' accounts. They should be set to the most commonly used VAT code, nominal code (N/C), department (if any) and discount rate. Most of these can be set by selecting from a drop-down list.

Statements

The Statements panel simply holds the descriptions to be applied to invoices, credit notes and other printouts.

Ageing

Chasing debts efficiently is a key part of good cashflow management. Aged Analysis groups overdue debts, with the default settings in multiples of 30 days. You can switch to calendar month grouping, or set your own limits. At which point do you start counting? How old is a debt before you send a reminder, and how much older before you send for the lawyers?

Discounts

If you have standard levels of sales at which you normally apply discounts, they can be set up here. Use the drop-down calculator, or type the values and the discount percentages.

Customer Defaults

Discount Type	Invoice Value	Discount %
Discount	250.00	2.50
Discount	1000.00	5.00
Discount	5000.00 7.50	
Discount	0.00	0.00
Discount	0.00	0.00
Discount	0.00	0.00
Discount	0.00	0.00
Discount	0.00	0.00
Discount	0.00	0.00
Discount	0.00	0.00

Tabs: Record | Statements | Ageing | **Discount**

Calculator keys: `<·` `C` `Ce` `/` `7` `8` `9` `*` `4` `5` `6` `·` `1` `2` `3` `+` `CC` `0` `.` `=`

OK   Cancel

Supplier Defaults

The Supplier Defaults dialog box only has the Record and Ageing panels, which are used as for Customer Defaults.

3.5 Bank accounts

Sage 50 comes with a basic set of bank accounts: current and deposit bank accounts, building society account, petty cash and company credit card. More can be set up if need be, and if you are likely to create more than a few, you might want to set the defaults. To do this:

1 *Open the* **Settings** *menu and select* **Bank Defaults...**
2 *Tick the checkboxes to turn the options on or off.*
  ▷ **Enable eBanking** *if you use online banking.*
  ▷ **Group items in Bank Rec.** *will display in one line any items where the reference code and date are the same.*
  ▷ **List Payment/Receipt by split** *shows the individual transactions in an invoice – this is turned on automatically if the company uses VAT cash accounting.*
  ▷ **No Warning on Visa receipts** *turns off the alert that appears if a receipt is entered against a company credit card account.*
  ▷ **Group Bank Transactions** *will group all of each day's bank transactions into a single header line.*
  ▷ **Always Create Remittance** *creates a remittance advice note when you record a supplier payment.*
3 *If you take money over the counter, check that the right Nominal codes are selected in the Cash register settings.*
4 *Click* **OK.**

Bank Defaults

General
- ☑ Enable e-Banking
- ☐ Group items in Bank Rec.
- ☑ List Payment/Receipt by split
- ☐ No Warning on Visa receipts
- ☑ Group Bank Transactions
- ☑ Always Create Remittance

Cash register settings
Bank A/C: 1235
Sales nominal: 4000
Tax code: T1 15.00
Discrepancies: 8206
☑ Takings are VAT inclusive

OK   Cancel

3.6 Products

The Product module provides stock control facilities, but the product information is also used when generating invoices and credit notes – selecting a product's code will pull in its description, price, tax rate and default order quantity. It can take time to enter the details of all your business's products, but it will save more time in the long run. You can speed up data entry by setting appropriate defaults for the products.

Products can be organized into categories. If you have a website where you display or sell your products, these can help your customers to locate items. They can also be useful for analysing your business activities.

If you intend to use categories, they are best created before setting the defaults and before entering the details of products.

1   *Open the Settings menu, select Configuration... and switch to the Products panel.*
2   *Select an unused category and click* **Edit**.

3 *Enter a name and click* **OK.**

Edit Product Category		X
No	4	
Name	Monitors	
	OK	Cancel

4 *Repeat steps 2 and 3 for all your new categories, then click Apply to store the definitions in your configuration data, or* **Save** *to save the new configuration to file.*

Product categories

If necessary, a new product category can be set up when you are creating a product record.

To set the product defaults:

1 *Open the* **Settings** *menu and select* **Product Defaults...**

Product Defaults	X
Details	Descriptions

Defaults	
Sales nominal code:	4000
Tax code:	T1 15.00
Purchase nominal code:	5000
Unit of sale:	Each
Category	1 Computer hardware
Department	1
Image options:	Maintain Image Size
EC VAT description:	

Decimal Precision	
Quantity D.P.	2
Unit D.P.	2

OK Cancel

2 *Select the most common settings for Nominal Code, Tax Code, Unit of Sale, Category and Department.*

3 *Set the number of decimal places to show for* **Quantities** *and* **Prices** *on invoices.*

4 *Click* **OK.**

3.7 Invoice and order defaults

There are six tabs of settings in the Invoice and Order Defaults dialog box. All need to be checked and changed to suit your business. In particular, you should set the default invoice to the type you use most – product or service, and if you have cash sales, you should select which printouts are to be produced with each sale.

1 *From the* **Settings** *menu select* **Invoice & Order Defaults...**

2 *On the* **General** *tab, set the default invoice and sales order format and their related options.*

3 *On the* **Footer Defaults**, *set the default net costs and nominal codes for carriage on sales and purchases.*

4 *On the* **Options** *tab, set the start points for numbering on the printouts if you want to pick up from existing sequences.*

5 *On the* **Discounts** *tab, set the defaults for how and to whom discounts are to apply.*

6 *If your trade within the EU requires it, switch to the* **Instrastat** *tab and turn on the reporting options.*

7 *If you have cash sales, go to the* **Cash Sales** *tab and set the printing options.*

8 *Click* **OK.**

3.8 Program Date

Whenever a date is required, the current date will be set as the default, but it can be easily changed. If you intend to process a

lot of transactions with the same date – and not today's – set the
Program Date before you start.

1 *Open the* **Settings** *menu and select* **Change Program Date...**
2 *Set the date, by typing or by using the calendar display.*

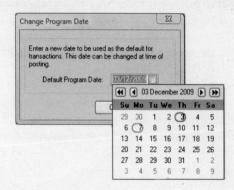

3 *Set the date and click* **OK.**

3.9 Change Password

If you need to protect your accounts, you can set a password to
be given at the start of every session. The password should be
something you won't forget, but one that others will not guess
easily. It should be changed regularly for optimum security.

1 *Open the* **Settings** *menu and select* **Change Password.**
2 *Type the password* twice – *as only asterisks are shown, this
   avoids mistyping errors.*

Change Password

Change Password

Logon Name	MANAGER
New Password	××××××
Confirm New Password	××××××

Discard　　OK　　Cancel

3 *In future, the password must be given at the start of each session, and must also be given if you want to change it.*

4 *If things change and a password is no longer needed, run the Change routine again, and leave the Password fields blank.*

THINGS TO REMEMBER

▶ To tailor Sage 50 to suit your business, you should start by working through the tabs of the Configuration Editor.

▶ The details of your business are recorded in the Company Preferences section. As with almost all of the Settings data, they can be changed at any time if necessary.

▶ If you set up defaults to suit the majority of your customers and suppliers, it will simplify life when you create new accounts.

▶ If you deal in products, you should set up suitable product defaults.

▶ Other options on the Settings menu let you change the program date, invoice and order defaults and the password.

4

The Company module

In this chapter you will learn:
- *about Company tasks and tools*
- *about the chart of accounts*
- *how to create Nominal accounts*
- *about journal entries*
- *how to view activity*
- *how to edit report layouts*

4.1 Company tasks and tools

The Company module covers all of the Nominal ledger work, except for those tasks that relate to any of the bank accounts. It is here that you define the structure of the accounts, set opening balances, make journal entries and reversals, compile the VAT return and manage your assets. The financial analysis tools and reports, and the end of period routines can also be reached from this module.

When you first open the Company module, the Nominal Ledger will appear. Accounts are grouped by type, with only the top level areas visible at first. Click on the Plus sign to expand an area – there will normally be a second level of grouping, so click again to display the individual accounts. The current balances of the accounts are shown, and the total balances in the groups. The sub-totals and totals of expanded areas are shown in blue to avoid confusion.

Some operations are started from the Tasks in the left-hand pane, others from the toolbar buttons – and some from both. There are also several buttons below the display of accounts:

▶ **Print List** *will give you a hard copy of the accounts' N/C (Nominal Code), names and balances;*
▶ **Expand all** *will open all areas fully;*
▶ **Collapse all** *will restore the display of top-level areas only.*

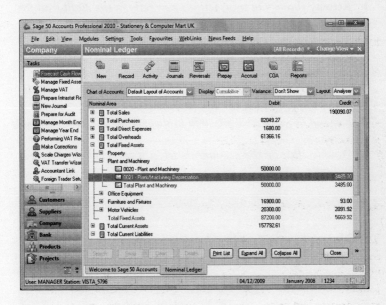

4.2 Nominal records

Though the Nominal ledger is the heart of the accounting system, once it is set up there are relatively few situations in which you will work on it directly. Most Nominal ledger entries arise from transactions with customers and suppliers, which are normally handled through the Bank (Chapter 7), Customers or Suppliers (Chapter 8) modules.

The Nominal module is mainly used for viewing Nominal records, for performing (fairly rare) journal entries, and for setting up budgets.

The record panels have four tabs:

▶ **Details** *shows the current balance, and the balance, budget and prior year figures for each month (if present).*
▶ **Graphs** *shows the same monthly figures in visual form.*
▶ **Activity** *shows the transactions currently in the audit trail for that account.*
▶ **Memo** *is a free space in which any notes can be written.*

To view records:
1 *Switch to the* **Company** *module. The* **Nominal Ledger** *will be open, showing a list of Nominal areas.*
2 *Expand the area and sub-area to display the account you want to see.*
3 *Double-click on the account or select it and click the* **Record** *button.*

Nominal Record - Creditors Control Account

| Details | Graphs | Activity | Memo |

N/C   2100
Name   Creditors Control Account
Balance   44502.68 Cr   Account Type   Control Account

Month	Actuals	Budgets	To end Dec 2007
B/F	7929.71 Cr	0.00	0.00
Jan	7929.72 Dr	0.00	0.00
Feb	15203.25 Cr	0.00	0.00
Mar	6630.74 Cr	0.00	0.00
Apr	22642.95 Cr	0.00	0.00
May	25.85 Cr	0.00	0.00
Jun	0.00	0.00	0.00
Jul	0.00	0.00	0.00
Aug	0.00	0.00	0.00
Sep	0.00	0.00	0.00
Oct	0.00	0.00	0.00
Nov	0.00	0.00	0.00
Dec	0.00	0.00	0.00
Future	0.00	0.00	0.00
Total	44502.68 Cr	0.00	0.00

| Save | Discard | Delete | Previous | Next | Print List | Close |

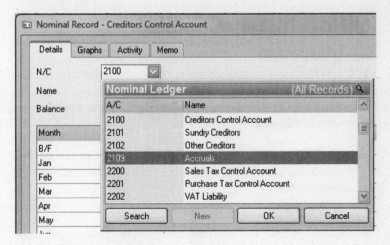

4 *Click on the headings to switch between the tabs.*
5 *Drop down the N/C list if you want to see the record for another account.*

6 *Click* **Close** *when done.*

Alternative views

By default, the Nominal ledger uses the Analyser layout, with accounts grouped into areas. There are two alternatives: List view shows all the accounts in nominal code order. Graph shows a pie chart, with each area of the ledger represented as a slice. Use Analyser layout when you want a structured view of the accounts; use List view when you want to select several accounts at a time for processing (you can't do this in Analyser layout). I haven't yet found a sensible use for Graph layout.

BUDGETS

If you want to include budget figures to help in analysing and monitoring your business's performance, they can be written into the Details tab of the Nominal Record window.

The budget data can be compared with the actual figures directly on the Details tab, or visually on the Graphs tab. The system can also produce a budget report, showing how far the actual figures differ from the budget, for the period and for the year to date.

To enter budget data:
  1 *Open the account in the* **Nominal Record** *window.*
  2 *Enter a budget figure for each month. Type this in directly or use the calculator buttons. (You can even use the calculator to work the amount.)*
or
  3 *Enter a figure for the year in the Total row. When you have finished, the system will offer to divide it equally between the months.*

Nominal Record – Sales North

Details | Graphs | Activity | Memo

N/C: 4000
Name: Sales North
Balance: 179507.53 C   Account Type: Control Account

Month	Actuals	Budgets	To end Dec 2007
B/F	0.00	0.00	0.00
Jan	39832.70 Cr	40000.00	0.00
Feb	37076.73 Cr		0.00
Mar	39705.77 Cr	0.00	0.00
Apr	47349.18 Cr	0.00	0.00
May	4500.00 Cr	0.00	0.00
Jun	416.70 Cr	0.00	0.00
Jul	4000.00 Cr	0.00	0.00
Aug	4833.40 Cr	0.00	0.00
Sep	0.00	0.00	0.00
Oct	1793.05 Cr	0.00	0.00
Nov	0.00	0.00	0.00
Dec	0.00	0.00	0.00
Future	0.00	0.00	0.00
Total	179507.53 Cr	40000.00	0.00

Save | Discard | Delete | Previous | Next | Print List | Close

---

4.3 Chart of Accounts

The Chart of Accounts is used by the Sage 50 system when
grouping and totalling accounts for calculating the Profit and
Loss account (page 186), and when producing the Balance Sheet
(page 188). A default chart is created when the software is
installed, with a structure to match the company configuration that
you selected (see page 59). It can be adjusted to suit the particular
needs of your business.

The default layout of the General configuration is summarized
below. Accounts are grouped into areas, which are then grouped
into category types. Each category will have a number of standard
accounts already in place, and these will normally occupy the first
few places in the number sequence. You can add new categories or
alter the ranges, to include different accounts.

The **Initial Range** shows the nominal codes currently grouped in each category type. In some cases, there are substantial gaps in a range. With sales, for instance, the main group falls between 4000 and 4299, but there are then sub-ranges for credit charges (4400–4499) and other sales (4900–4999), leaving big gaps where other categories could be inserted if needed. Where a category type has sub-ranges, these are shown below in lighter type.

The **Maximum** shows the highest code that can be included in the category type – the next one is the first in another type.

Category type	Initial range	Maximum
Fixed Assets	0010–0059	0999
Current Assets	1000–1250	1999
Current Liabilities	2100–2299	2299
Long Term Liabilities	2300–2399	2999
Capital & Reserves	3000–3299	3999
Sales	4000–4299	4399
Credit charges	4400–4499	4899
Other sales	4900–4999	
Purchases	5000–5299	5999
Direct Expenses	6000–6299	6999
Miscellaneous Expenses	6900–6999	
Overheads	7000–8299	9997
Suspense & Mispostings	9998–9999	

Default layout of the General configuration.

Note that the Bank accounts (1200–1209) and VAT liability (2200–2209) categories float between the assets and liabilities type depending upon whether they hold credit or debit balances.

To edit the chart of accounts:
1 *In the* **Company** *module, click the* **COA** *button.*
2 *Select a* **Layout** *– there may only be one – and click* **Edit***.*
3 *Click on a type to display its categories.*

To adjust a range:

4 *Type the new* **High** *code for the* **Category,** *or click on the down arrow and select the new highest account.*

To add a category:

5 *Type a suitable name.*
6 *Type the* **Low** *and* **High** *codes, or select them from the lists.*
7 *Click* **Save.**

Edit Chart of Accounts

Title

Default Layout of Accounts

Category Type

Category Type	Description
Sales	Sales
Purchases	Purchases
Direct Expenses	Direct Expenses
Overheads	Overheads
Fixed Assets	Fixed Assets
Current Assets	Current Assets
Current Liabilities	Current Liabilities
Long Term Liabilities	Long Term Liabilities
Capital & Reserves	Capital & Reserves

Category Account

Sales	Low	High
Product Sales	4000	4099
Export Sales	4100	4109
Sales of Assets	4200	4299
Credit Charges (Late Payments)	4400	4499
Other Sales	4900	4999
Royalties	4110	4120

Print   Check   Save   Close

8 *Close the* **Edit** *panel to return to the* **Chart of Accounts** *panel, and click* **Close** *to end.*

HAND-MADE CHARTS

If none of the ready-made charts of accounts are close enough to your needs, you can create your own from scratch.

1 *Click* **Add** *to start, and enter a name at the prompt.*
2 *When the* **Edit Chart of Accounts** *dialog box opens, the category types will be in place already but they will all be empty. Create your categories, with suitable ranges, for each type.*

Check and print

The Edit Chart of Accounts dialog box does not give you a clear overview of the whole chart, and this can lead to errors. You may find it useful – especially if you are creating a new chart or making major changes, to print the chart – click **Print** to get a hard copy. And after making any changes, however small, always click **Check** to get the system to check for overlapping ranges and other errors.

4.4 Editing the Nominal accounts

During installation, Sage 50 creates an extensive and well-organized set of nominal accounts, tailored to your type of business (see page 91). This may suit your needs with little or no adjustment, but can be changed easily – unwanted accounts can be deleted or their names edited, or new ones created.

The accounts most likely to need some attention are:

▶ *Stock accounts (numbered from 1000), Sales (4000 onwards) and Purchases (5000 onwards) may well need renaming to suit your types of goods or services.*

▶ *Overheads (7000 onwards) should be checked to see that they agree with your categories of expenses.*

▶ *You may want to handle computer hardware separately from other office equipment (N/C 0030), as it can be written off in two years, rather than the standard 25% p.a. of other capital equipment. This will require two accounts, which might be named 'Computer Hardware' and 'Computer Depreciation'.*

When replacing a default account with your own at the same place in the nominal structure, you can do this by editing the name or by deleting the old one and creating a new one. Do whichever is easier for you.

Some accounts may seem to be unnecessary. Don't delete any unless you are very clear about their intended use and that you do not need them. An empty account takes up a tiny amount of disk space.

Delete with care!

This is your second warning, because it is rather important. When a record has been selected it stays selected – so that multiple selections can be made. To be safe, click **Clear** to deselect all records before selecting any for deletion.

To edit the accounts:

1 *Switch to the* **Company** *module to display the nominal accounts list.*

2 *Click on the account(s) you want to change or delete.*

To edit the name:

3 *Double-click on the account or right-click on it and select* **Edit record...** *from the pop-up menu.*
4 *At the record window, edit the* **Name** *as required.*
5 *Save the new name.*

Where did it go?

When you click Save, the details of the account disappear – don't worry about this! The panel has been cleared ready for work on another account. This can be selected from the list that drops down from the N/C (Nominal Code) field.

6 *Click* **Close** *to close the record window and return to the main display.*
7 *Click on the record(s) again, or click* **Clear** *to deselect.*

To delete an account:

8 *Make sure that the only accounts selected are those that you want to delete.*

9 *Click* **Delete** *then confirm at the prompt.*

CREATING ACCOUNTS

When creating a new account, the key point to bear in mind is its location in the chart of accounts. The account must go within the range of the appropriate type – or just outside if the range can be extended to include it. If there is an appropriate category with an unused Nominal code, that is the ideal location.

1 *Click* **New.** *This will start the Nominal Record Wizard.*

2 *At the opening stage, click* **Next** *to get started.*

3 *Type a* **Name** *for the account, then select a* **Type** *from the list. Click* **Next.**

4 *Select a Category (from the Chart of Accounts – see below). The next available Nominal Code in that category will be allocated to the account. If you do not want the allocated Ref number, change it – but be sure it is in the right range. Click* **Next.**

Nominal Record Wizard

Nominal Information

Entering your nominal code name and type.

To create a new nominal account, you need to enter the nominal accounts name and select the type of nominal account that you are creating.

Name: Programming services

Type: Sales

- Sales
- Purchase
- Direct Expenses
- Overheads

Cancel   Help   Back   Next   Finish

Nominal Record Wizard

Nominal Information

Entering your nominal category and account code.

The new nominal account can be given a category within the chart of accounts and a unique reference code to identify the account.

Category: Other Sales

Ref: 4904

Cancel   Help   Back   Next   Finish

---

5 *You will be asked if you want to enter an opening balance. Select* **Yes** *if you do, then click* **Next**.

6 *Enter the Date and Amount, and check that the default Debit/ Credit selection is appropriate. (See the next section for more on opening balances.) Click* **Next**.

7 *At the final stage, click* **Finish** *to create the new record.*

New accounts and the chart of accounts

If you create new accounts you may need to adjust the ranges or set up new categories. This can be done before or after creating the accounts.

4.5 Double-entry bookkeeping

When you start to use Sage 50 in earnest, you will find that with day-to-day transactions – sales, purchases and payments – you only need to record the details of each transaction once. When you are recording receipt of a payment, for example, you simply tell the system which account the money is going into, which customer has paid which invoice and how much is received. The system then handles the double-entry bookkeeping for you.

It doesn't always work this way. With some transactions you have to make the double entries yourself, and the first time you will come across these is when recording opening balances.

OPENING BALANCES

When you transfer to the Sage system, opening balances (O/B) should normally be entered on all accounts where transactions have taken place. In an ongoing business this will probably mean all used accounts, except those of suppliers and customers where debts have been cleared. If the business is just being started up, you will still need to enter opening balances in the Capital and Bank accounts, and perhaps those for property and other assets.

Opening balances may also be needed when you create new accounts. This is less likely with customers and suppliers, where you will normally set up the account with a zero balance before you begin to record your transactions.

Every opening balance must have an equivalent entry in another account – every debit needs a balancing credit, and vice versa. Remember:

▶ **Debit**: *movement of value into an account.*
▶ **Credit**: *movement of value out of an account.*

e.g. when you have bought something, it will be entered as a debit in the appropriate asset, purchase or expense account and a credit in a bank or supplier's account.

The best way to record an opening balance is through the new account wizard or through a record window, as we are doing here. In either case, this will automatically make the balancing entry in the *Suspense* account (N/C 9998), which serves as a temporary home for values. You then have to make a journal entry to move the value from there to its proper home – typically the current or other bank account. This is not difficult, and there are simple ways to ensure that you get it right.

To enter a balance in an existing account:
1 *In the appropriate module, locate the record(s) to be edited. Double-click it, or click **Record** if several are selected, to open the record window.*
2 *Click on the **Balance** field.*
3 *Set the **Date**.*
4 *Enter the value into the **Debit** or **Credit** field. (Remember, if value is coming into the account, e.g. you're recording the purchase of goods or services, then it's a debit.)*
5 *Click **Save**.*
    ▷ *If several records have been selected, click **Next** to go to the next, and repeat steps 2 to 5.*
6 *Click **Close** to close the record window.*
7 *Back at the Nominal accounts display, scroll to the bottom of the list. You should see that the Suspense account contains an amount equivalent (but opposite) to the opening balance(s). This needs to be moved into the appropriate account(s), and to do that we use journal entries.*

4.6 Journal entries

A journal entry is a transfer between Nominal accounts. Typical uses include relocating amounts placed in Suspense, and recording depreciation or the revaluation of stock or other assets.

Making a journal entry is one of the few situations where you have to do the double-entry bookkeeping yourself, rather than leaving it to the system. An entry normally consists of a pair of transactions, one debit, one credit. Sometimes there will be more than two, but the total debits and credits must always balance – you cannot save the entries until it does!

Before you start, make a note of the details of the monies to be moved – the source and target accounts, date, reference and amount.

1 *Click* **Journals** *to open the Nominal Ledger Journals window.*

2 *Give a* **Reference** *to identify the journal.*
3 *Set the* **Date.**
4 *Set the N/C number of the Nominal account into which the value will be moved from Suspense.*
5 *Type the* **Details.**
6 *Enter the amount in the* **Debit** *or* **Credit** *column – this should be the same side as the original Suspense entry.*
7 *Repeat steps 4 to 6 for the balancing entry to move the amount out of the Suspense account – this will be the opposite debit/credit to the original.*
8 *If there are several opening balances to correct, repeat steps 2 to 7 for each of them.*
9 *Click* **Save.** *If the total debit and credit entries are not the same, you will be told so. You can only save and exit from the journals window when the entries balance.*

REVERSALS

You shouldn't normally need to use these, but it's good to know that the possibility exists. If you discover that a journal entry has been made in error, you can undo it with a reversal.

Before making the reversal, you should ensure the safety of your data. Print out a day book report (see page 103), then run a check on your data and back it up. The system will prompt you to do this.

1 *In the Nominal ledger display, click* **Reversals**.
2 *You will be prompted to print the Day Book report and to back up – do so now if you have not already done so.*
3 *At the* **Transaction Range** *dialog box, set the* **Range***, the* **Date** *and/or* **Reference** *– any or all will filter the display to make it easier to find the transaction you want to reverse.*

Transaction Range	X

Select a range of transaction numbers, posting date, posting reference or posting department to be selected for reversal.

Transaction Range

From: 1218

To: 1238

Posting Information

Date: 01/01/2010

Reference:

Department: 0

OK	Cancel

4 *Select the pair(s) of transactions to reverse.*
5 *Click* **Reverse***. If the totals of the debit and credit transactions do not balance, you will not be allowed to go any further.*
6 *The system will generate the reversing transactions and display them. Click* **Save** *to make the changes.*

Nominal Reversals

No	N/C	Type	Date	Ref.	Details	Amount	Debit	Credit
1235	4904	JD	01/01/2010	O/Bal	Opening Balance	2400.00	2400.00	
1236	9998	JC	01/01/2010	O/Bal	Opening Balance	2400.00		2400.00

2400.00   2400.00
0.00

Range   Reverse   Cancel

Nominal Reversals

N/C	Name	Date	Dept	Details	T/C	Debit	Credit
4904	Programming services	01/01/2010	0	Reversal of Tran. 1...	T9		2400.00
9998	Suspense Account	01/01/2010	0	Reversal of Tran. 1...	T9	2400.00	

2400.00   2400.00

Save   Cancel

4.7 Activity

If your main interest in the Nominal accounts is in the transactions,
you may prefer to view them through the Activity display. The same
information is shown as in the Activity tab of the record panel, but
you can move more easily between different records here. You can
look at the transactions in a preselected set of accounts, and/or select
individual accounts once you are in the Activity display window.

Before the window opens, you will have the opportunity to limit the display by setting the number range, types or date limits of the transactions.

1 *If you want to look at specific records, select them first.*
2 *Click* **Activity**.

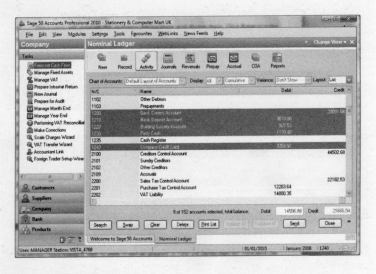

3 *Limit the display, if required, by setting a month, quarter or other period from the* **Show** *list. This also has a Custom option where you can specify the date range and transaction type.*
4 *At the Activity window, select a transaction to see its components (if any) in the lower pane.*
5 *Move through the preselected accounts using the* **Previous** *and* **Next** *buttons, or*
6 *Select an account from the drop-down list.*
7 *Click* **Close** *when you have done.*

4.8 Reports

Sage 50 has ready-made reports for many purposes. In the Nominal module alone there are nearly 20, grouped into eight sets:

▶ **Day Books:** *lists journal entries and reversals.*
▶ **Departmental:** *analyses nominal accounts by departments.*
▶ **My Nominal Reports:** *lists any that you create yourself, either from scratch or by adapting existing reports.*
▶ **Nominal Activity:** *shows the transactions in each Nominal account – with or without inactive accounts.*
▶ **Nominal Balances:** *lists the balance in each account.*
▶ **Nominal Budgets:** *budget reports for the year, half-year or quarter.*
▶ **Nominal Details:** *list the Nominal accounts, with or without monthly values. Two of these are in CSV (Comma Separated Values) format, which can be read by most databases and spreadsheets. Use it if you want to process the data further using one of these applications.*

▶ **Nominal Quick Ratio**: *lists the assets and liabilities accounts and shows the credit/debit balance (see page 17).*

Most reports can list all the accounts or those in a selected range. Depending upon the type of report, this can be based on the nominal code, date, transaction number or department.

1 *Click* **Reports** *to open the Report Browser.*

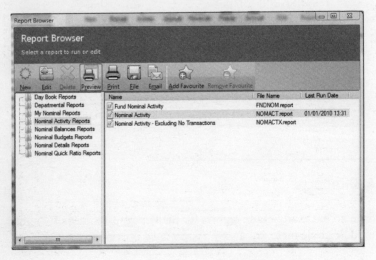

2 *Select a set in the left-hand pane, then select a layout.*
3 *Choose the output from the toolbar – Preview, Print, File or E-mail.*
4 *In the* **Criteria** *dialog box, you can specify a range of nominal codes, transaction dates or numbers.*
5 *If you are outputting to printer, it's wise to check that the criteria select the right things, so set a number to preview – two or three are often enough.*
6 *Click* **OK** *to generate the report.*

Criteria

Criteria Values

Enter the values to use for the criteria in this report

Nominal Code	Between (inclusive) ▼	1001 Stock ▼	and	2330 Mortgages ▼
Transaction Date	Between (inclusive) ▼	01/01/2009 ▼	and	01/08/2009 ▼
Transaction No	All ▼			
Inc B/Fwd Tran	☐			

Preview a sample report for a specified number of records or transactions (0 for all)   0

Help   OK   Cancel

EDITING A REPORT

Predefined reports can be edited to your requirements. If you
worked through the example in Chapter 2 and used the Report
Designer to produce a letter from scratch, then you should have no
trouble in editing.

1 *At the* **Nominal Reports** *dialog box, select an existing report and click* **Edit.** *The* **Report Designer** *window will open.*

Notice the headings above each area. These vary, and include:

- ▶ **Report Header** – *anything in this area goes at the start of the report.*
- ▶ **Page Header** – *anything here will appear at the top of every page.*
- ▶ **Subsection Header** – *material to appear at the start of each account, department, category or whatever divisions apply.*
- ▶ **Details** – *this line is repeated for all transactions in each account.*
- ▶ **Footers** – *printed at the end of each account.*
- ▶ **Report Footer** – *appears only on the last page of the report.*

2 If you want to add anything to an area, you may need to make more space. Click on the line at the bottom of the area and drag it down.

3 Lines, boxes, images and text boxes can be added from the Toolbox – click on its tab on the far left to open it. Variables can be selected from the Variable list, also opened from a tab on the left. Add your material as shown in Chapter 2 (page 38).

4 Click the **Preview** button on the toolbar to see the effects of your changes.

5 When you are done, use **File > Save As** to save the edited report with a new name – it will be listed with the other My Nominal Reports.

Print margins

If your printer's page set up does not match the printout's set up, you'll get an error message – use the Fix option, and let the system sort things out!

THINGS TO REMEMBER

▶ *The Company module covers most of the activities relating to Nominal accounts.*

▶ *The basic Nominal accounts have been created for you. Unwanted ones can be deleted and new ones created to suit your business.*

▶ *The Chart of Accounts creates the structure for calculating the Profit and Loss account and Balance Sheet.*

▶ *When you set up accounts, you can enter opening balances at the time.*

▶ *If wanted, budget figures can be entered for each month in Nominal accounts. Comparing these with actual figures can be instructive.*

▶ *Journal entries are used to transfer value between Nominal accounts. Recording depreciation is a typical use for them.*

▶ *The Activity tab offers the best way to view Nominal account transactions.*

▶ *The reports available from the Company module include simple and grouped lists of transactions and summaries of account balances.*

5

Customers and suppliers

In this chapter you will learn:
- *how to create records for customers and suppliers*
- *about viewing and editing records*
- *how to search for records*
- *about printouts*

5.1 New records

In the Sage 50 systems, customers and suppliers are handled in almost identical ways, as you might expect – it is the same trading relationship, but viewed from opposite ends. The examples in this chapter are drawn from the Customers module, but – with rare exceptions – could have come from the Suppliers.

Accounts can be set up from the **New** button in the customers/ suppliers list in those windows that handle invoices, receipts and payments – a blank record opens to take the details. However, the simplest way is to use the New Wizard in the Customers and Suppliers modules. This helps to ensure that all essential information is entered, and creates an A/C (account) reference for you.

1 *Open the* **Customer** *module and click* **New**.
2 *Click* **Next** *to get started, and* **Next** *after each stage.*
3 *Enter the* **Name**. *An* **A/C Ref** *will be generated – edit this to make it easier to recognize, if necessary.*

Customer Record Wizard

Customer Information

Entering your Customers name and unique reference.

To create a new customer account you need to enter the customer's name and a unique reference.

Name   Data Recovery Ltd

A/C Ref   DATARECO

Cancel   Help   Back   Next   Finish

4 *Enter the* **Address details.**
5 *Enter the* **Contact details** *and set the* **Account Status –** *normally* **Open** *(active, existing client) or* **New.**

Customer Record Wizard

Customer Information

Entering address details
Now enter your customer's address details.

Street1	12 The Avenue
Street2	
Town	Northampton
County	
Post Code	NN2 5TH`
Country	United Kingdom GB
Telephone	0255 512345
Fax	0255 512346

Cancel   Help   Back   Next   Finish

6 *At the three* **Additional Information** *stages, check and adjust the* **Credit Limit** *and* **Terms** *as required. If terms have been agreed with the customer, tick the checkbox at the second stage – until this is ticked, you will get a reminder every time you open the account.*

Customer Record Wizard

Customer Information

Entering contact information about your customer.

Email	erica.ling@datarecovery.co.uk
Website	
Contact Name	Erica Ling
Trade Contact	
VAT Number	679 3251 07
Account Status	08 - New

Cancel   Help   Back   Next   Finish

Customer Record Wizard

Customer Information

Entering Additional Information (1)

Use the following screens to enter additional customer details.

Credit Limit	500.00	Nominal Code	4002
Discount %	5.00	Use Default Nominal Code for Sales	☐
Additional Discount	No additional	Tax Code	T 1 17.50
Currency	1 - Pound Sterling	Use Default Tax Code for Sales	☐

Cancel   Help

Customer Record Wizard

Customer Information

Entering Additional Information (2)

Settlement Due Days	0	Sett.Disc %	2.50
Payment Due Days	30		
Terms	30 Days Strictly Net		
Terms Agreed	☐ ?		

Cancel   Help   Back   Next   Finish

7 *Enter the customer's bank details, if payments are to be by BACS.*

8 *If you are bringing an existing customer onto the system, you may need to set the* **opening balance.** *This can be entered as a set of individual transactions, or as a single value.*

Missing details?

If you do not have all the required information about the new customer, or do not have time to fill it in at that point, you can reopen the record and enter the missing details at any time.

5.2 Viewing and editing records

The record displays for customers and suppliers show not simply their contact details and terms of trade, but also the flow of business to date and the current state of their accounts.

You can edit the information on the Details, Defaults, Credit Control, Contacts and Memo tabs. The details on the other tabs can only be viewed and not edited.

1 *Double-click on the record you want to view or edit*
or
2 *Select several records and click* **Record.**

THE RECORD WINDOW BUTTONS

The Previous and Next buttons are only available if several records were selected before opening the window.

▸ **Save** *writes any changes into the file.*
▸ **Discard** *restores the record to how it was before the changes.*
▸ **Delete** *deletes the whole* **record,** *not a transaction. To delete a transaction, use the Corrections routine (see page 47).*

- ▶ **Previous** *where several records have been selected, this opens the one above in the list.*
- ▶ **Next** *opens the next record in the list.*
- ▶ **New Order** *opens the sales order window.*
- ▶ **New Invoice** *opens the Invoicing window.*
- ▶ **New Project** *opens the Project Record window.*
- ▶ **Close** *closes the record window.*

VIEWING SALES ACTIVITY

You can view the trading activity with your customers in several different ways.

- ▶ *On the* **Sales** *tab, you can see a summary of the invoices, credits, balances and receipts for each month, and the details behind each of these figures can be displayed if required. Double-click on a cell to display its details window, then click on the plus sign to open up any item. Click* **Close** *to return to the main display.*

▶ On the **Orders** tab you can see the status of current and recent orders.

▶ If you organize and invoice any of your sales through projects, current and recent ones are listed on the **Projects** tab.

▶ The **Activity** tab lists all the transactions to date, back to the point when the audit trail was last cleared (see page 181). A busy account can produce a long list of transactions. If you don't want to struggle through the list, use the **Show** options to restrict the display to a set period, or a custom range of time and/or transaction type.

▶ Select a transaction in the top pane to see its details in the lower pane.

▶ The **Graphs** tab is perhaps the most complex. It deserves a closer look.

Credit control

We'll come back to the record window and look at the Credit Control tab in Chapter 7, Credit Control.

GRAPHS

Graphs can help to show underlying trends that are not immediately visible from the raw data. With the right sort of graph – bar chart, pie chart, line, scatter or Hi-Lo graph – presented in the right way, you can see relationships and changes over time, much more clearly than you can by poring over sets of numbers. On the other hand, you can spend an awful lot of time trying out different display modes and tweaking the layout and design – and not have much to show for it at the end of the day.

I suspect that, in most firms, the trading patterns with their regular customers/suppliers follow fairly simple trends or seasonal fluctuations, which will show up on simple line, area or bar chart, and little that is useful will come out of any of the more esoteric display modes.

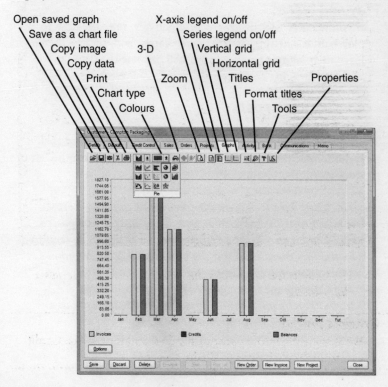

1 *Switch to the* **Graphs** *tab.*
2 *Select a* **type**.
3 *Experiment with the tools to see what they do and find settings that you like.*

and/or

4 *Click the Properties button to open the* **Chart Properties** *dialog box and set the options there.*

Play and learn!

If you want to use the graphs productively, take the time to play with the settings until you are happy with them – then leave them alone. These settings will become the defaults for all future graphs.

COPYING GRAPH DATA

There are two ways in which the graph can be copied and then pasted into another application. Notice these buttons on the left of the toolbar on the Graphs tab.

▶ *The* **Copy data** *tool copies the figures on which the graph is based to the Clipboard as text. They can then be pasted into a word-processor or spreadsheet. Try not to be confused by the fact that the icon is the one used in other Windows applications for the* **Cut** *operation!*

▶ *The* **Copy image** *tool captures the graph as a picture. It can then be pasted into a graphics application, or to a word-processor that can handle images.*

5.3 Searching

If you only have a few customers and suppliers, and are reasonably familiar with the state of their accounts, it's no great bother to run through the list selecting them individually when you want to examine or process them. Once you get beyond a few, it's worth learning how to use the Search routine.

By specifying criteria, you can pick out those accounts where the values in a field match a given value. For example:

▶ *the customers in a town,*
▶ *the suppliers whose invoices are due,*
▶ *trading partners where the annual turnover is over £10,000 or those below £500.*

Conditions can be set on as many fields as necessary, to select very specific sets of records. Conditions can be joined by **And**, if both must apply, or **Or**, where records are selected if either or both conditions apply.

The example here is from the Customer module, but the Search routine is used in the same way in all modules.

1 *Click* **Search***.*
2 *In the* **Join** *column, select* **Where***.*
3 *Click into the* **Field** *column and select a field from the list.*
4 *Click into the* **Condition** *column and select one.*
5 *Type the* **Value***.*
6 *If you want to set another condition, click into the Join box of the next line and select* **And** *or* **Or***, then work through steps 3 to 5 again.*
7 *Click* **Apply***, then* **Close***. The customer list will now only display those records that match the criteria.*

Search –

Only select records from 'Customers'

Join	Field	Condition	Value
Where	Registered Address Line4	Is Equal To	Tyne & Wear
And	Credit Limit	Is Greater Than Or Equal To	2000.00

<<New>>
And
Or

Expression:

Where 'Registered Address Line4' = 'Tyne & Wear' And 'Credit Limit' >= '2000.00'

[Wizard] [Discard] [Open] [Save] [Save As] [Apply] [Close]

Sage 50 Accounts Professional 2010 - Stationery & Computer Mart UK

File   Edit   View   Modules   Settings   Tools   Favourites   WebLinks   News Feeds   Help

Customers

Tasks
- New Customer
- Edit Customer
- Chase Debt
- New Quotation
- New Sales Order
- New Invoice
- Allocate Stock
- Despatch Orders
- Receive Payment
- Post Invoices
- New Credit
- Customer Write Off/Refund
- Customer Refund
- New Diary Event

Customers
Suppliers
Company
Bank
Products

New   Record   Price List   Activity   Aged   Invoice   Credit   Dispute   Charges   Labels   Letters

A/C	Name	Balance	Credit Limit	Contact	Telephone
ABS001	ABS Garages Ltd	2533.31	4000.00	Mike Hall	0191 254 5909
COM001	Compton Packaging	2807.04	4000.00	Sean Morris	0191 121 9876
KIN001	Kingham & French	7396.35	6000.00	John Bell	0191 676 5656
SDE001	S D Enterprises	15339.68	5000.00	Jane Scott	0191 937 9836
SWA001	Swan Leisure Centre	1598.83	4000.00	John Blair	0191 567 2345

0 of 5 customers selected, total balance   0.00

[Search] [Swap] [Clear] [Delete] [Print List] [Duplicate] [Batch Change]   [Close]

User: MANAGER Station: VISTA_4892   02/01/2010   January 2008   1241

8 *To display all the records again, reopen the* **Search** *dialog box and click* **Discard**, *to clear the search criteria, then* **Apply** *and* **Close**.

The search wizard

If you prefer, you can set up the search through a wizard.
The results are exactly the same – it just walks you through
the steps given above. Click **Search** to open the dialog
box, then click **Wizard** to start.

5.4 Customer reports

There are twelve sets of ready-made reports that can be obtained from the Customer module.

▶ *The* **Customer Details** *and* **Sales Contacts** *reports are useful practical summaries, while the* **Top Customer** *reports highlight the ones to look after.*
▶ *The* **Customer Activity, Daily Transaction, Day Book, Departmental** *and* **EC Sales** *reports provide a range of ways to view and analyse your trading patterns.*

We'll come back to the **Customer Invoice** reports in Chapter 6 and the **Aged Debtor** and **Credit control** reports in Chapter 7.

To produce a report:

1 *Click* **Reports** *to open the Report Browser.*

2 *Select a set in the left-hand pane, then select a layout.*
3 *Choose the output: Printer, Preview, File or E-mail.*

4 *In the* **Criteria** *dialog box, you can define a range of accounts. You may also be able to set a range of dates, transaction numbers and/or nominal codes, depending upon the report.*

5 *If you are outputting to printer, set a number to preview a sample.*

Criteria					×
Criteria Values					
Enter the values to use for the criteria in this report					
Customer Ref	Between (inclusive) ▾	DATARECO Data Rec ▾	and	MIL001 Mile Road H ▾	
Next Credit Review Date	Between (inclusive) ▾	02/12/2009 ▾	and	02/01/2010 ▾	
Preview a sample report for a specified number of records or transactions (0 for all)			2 ▾		
Help				OK	Cancel

6 *Click* **OK** *to generate the report.*

As with Nominal reports, if there isn't one that meets your requirements, you can edit an existing one, or create a report from scratch (see section 2.9).

5.5 Statements and labels

STATEMENTS

In addition to reports, the Customers and Suppliers modules also have a selection of ready-made labels, letters and statements, some designed for output onto plain paper, others onto Sage stationery. Here's how statements can be produced:

1 *Select the customer(s) to whom you want to send the statements. (If you want to send them to all customers or to a continuous set from the customer list, do not select any.)*

2 *Click* **Statement.**

3 *Select the layout – and note that there are different sizes of paper as well as styles of statement.*

4 *Choose the output: Printer, Preview, File or E-mail.*

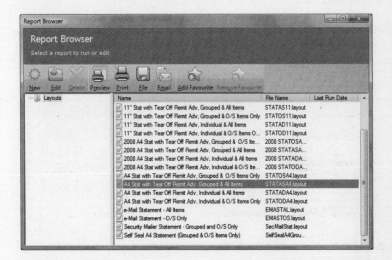

5 *At the* **Criteria** *dialog box, leave the* **Customer Ref** *fields alone if you selected accounts in step* 1. *Set a range of* **Transaction Dates** *if this will be useful, or leave at the defaults to include all current transactions.*

6 *Set a number to preview if you want to check the outputs.*

7 *Click* **OK** *to generate the report.*

LABELS

With labels, the procedure is the same, but you will probably need to change the Page Setup to suit your labels. Sage 50 knows some standard labels, and you can easily define your own.

1 *Select the customer(s), if appropriate, then click* **Labels**.
2 *The Report Browser window will open. Select the layout – sales or delivery, for 12" or A4 sheets.*

3 *Click* **Edit** *to take it into Report Designer.*
4 *Open the* **Format** *menu and select* **Labels & Forms**.
5 *At the* **Label Details** *dialog box, select a* **Preset** *label size, or click the* **Advanced** *button and define the label size and layout.*
6 *After editing, save the design and close Report Designer.*

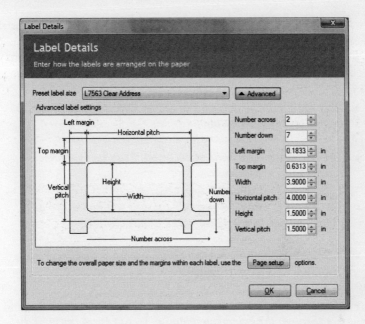

7 *Back at the **Labels** dialog box, select the output mode and continue as for statements.*

Supplier printouts

The Supplier module has an almost identical range of reports, letters and labels – though no statements, of course – as the Customer module.

SUMMARY

▶ New customer and supplier accounts are easily set up using the Wizard.

▶ Records can be viewed and edited by selecting them from the list in the module window.

▶ The current transactions in an account can be examined through the Activity tab.

▶ The monthly totals through an account can be viewed as graphs, which may help to make trends clearer.

▶ A Search will let you control which accounts and records are displayed in a module window.

▶ If invoices and credit notes have been produced manually, and not through the Invoicing window, record them through the Invoices and Credit routines.

▶ Statements can be easily printed whenever they are needed.

▶ Most printouts are designed for use with Sage pre-printed stationery. You can edit layouts in the Report Designer.

6

....

Invoices

In this chapter you will learn:
* *how to produce invoices*
* *about credit notes*
* *how to update ledgers*
* *about batch invoices*
* *about recurring invoices*

6.1 Invoicing in Sage 50

The tools in the Invoicing window can be used to create, edit and print invoices, credit notes, labels and reports, and to post the transactions to the appropriate accounts in the Customers and Nominal ledgers.

▶ *To open the Invoicing window, click* **Modules** *in the menu bar and select* **Invoicing**.

There are different invoice structures for products and services. When creating a product invoice, on each item line you select a product from your stock list and enter how many. The system then fills in the details, unit price and total cost for you. With a service invoice you have to type in the details and work out the costs yourself.

When a sale involves both materials and labour, there are two possible solutions:

▶ *Set up labour as a 'Product', with the sales price being the hourly rate. You may need several records for different types of skilled and unskilled labour. The job can then be processed through a product invoice.*
▶ *Include materials in the details of a service invoice. The catches with this are that you will have to calculate material costs, and that product elements will not be posted automatically to the relevant Nominal accounts.*

PRODUCT INVOICES

The basic design of an invoice is the same whether it is for a product or a service. There are always:

▶ *Invoice No. – generated automatically.*
▶ *Date – also set for you, but can be changed if necessary.*

- ▶ *A/C Ref – selecting this pulls the name and address into the heading area on the top left.*
- ▶ *Order No. – if the customer has given one.*
- ▶ *VAT and the Totals – calculated by the system.*

In a Product invoice you also need to specify the items and the quantity of each.

1 *Open the* **Invoicing** *module, make sure that no existing invoices are selected and click the* **New/Edit** *button.*
2 *If* Product *is not the default* **Format***, select it.*
3 *Set the* **Date***.*
4 *Enter an* **Order No.** *if required.*
5 *Select the* **A/C** *code from the list. The customer's details will be copied into the address block in the top left.*

6 *For a defined product, select its* **Code** *from the drop-down list; its* **Description** *and* **Price** *will be written in for you. If it is not in the list, click* **New** *and add it to your stock list now.*

Products   (All Records)

Code	Name
TR002	LP200 Laser Printer Toner
TR003	JP010 Jet Printer Cartridge
TR004	JP020 Jet Printer Cartridge
TR005	JP030 Jet Printer Cartridge
TRAY001	Letter Trays - 3 pack (Black)
TRAY002	Letter Trays - 3 pack (Pink/Brown)
TRAY003	Letter Trays - 3 pack (Grey)

[Search] [New] [OK] [Cancel]

7 *Enter the* **Quantity.** *The* **Net** *will then be calculated.*

8 *If you want to edit the description, add a comment, or change the price or other aspect, click the arrow icon by the* **Description** *field to open the* **Edit Item Line** *dialog box.*

Edit Item Line

Details

Product Code	PRN002	Units: Each
Description	LP200 Laser Printer	
Comment 1		
Comment 2		
Order Reference		Order Line Reference: 0

Values

Quantity	1.00	Discount %	5.0000	Net GBP £	1140.00
Unit Price GBP £	1200.00	Disc. GBP £	60.00	VAT GBP £	194.51

Posting Details

Nominal Code	4000	Department	1
Tax Code	T1 17.50		

Additional Information

Line Information

[Calc. Net] [Discounts] [Price List]   [OK] [Cancel]

9 *Edit or add details as required – to give a* **Discount,** *enter either the percentage or the actual amount. Click* **OK** *when you have done to return to the Invoice window.*

10 *Repeat steps 7 to 9 for each item. If the running total triggers a new discount level, you will be alerted.*

11 *Click* **Save**.

12 *Repeat steps 2 to 8 if you have other invoices to create, then click* **Close**.

FURTHER DETAILS

Many invoices can be completed simply using the top panel. The other panels allow you to add or adjust the details.

▶ Use the **Order Details** *panel to change the delivery address or contact details from the defaults, or to add any notes.*

▶ Use the **Footer Details** *panel to add a carriage charge, or alter the default charge, or to adjust discounts and terms.*

▶ *If a payment has been received, this can be recorded on the* **Payment Details** *tab. The money can be allocated to that invoice, or as a general payment to the account.*

If you use couriers who offer parcel tracking through their websites, add their names and site details to the Couriers list – use Settings > Internet Resources to reach this list.

To change the carriage and terms:

1 *Switch to the* **Footer Details** *panel.*
2 *Enter the* **Carriage** *details – costs, codes and courier if used.*
3 *Adjust the* **Terms** *as needed.*

To record payments:

1 *Switch to the* **Payment Details** *panel.*

2 *Enter the* **Ref** *and* **Amount.**
3 *Set any payment against the* **account** *or the* **invoice.**

Is it worth it?

Notice the **Profit** button at the bottom of the Invoice window.
Click on this to find out how much profit the business will
make from the sale.

SERVICE INVOICES

1 *Begin as for a product invoice (page 128), but select* Service *as the* Format.
2 *Type the* Details.
3 *Enter the* Amount.
4 *To add an item, press* [Tab] *or click into the next blank line and repeat steps 2 and 3.*
5 *Click* Save.

6.2 Credit notes

Credit notes are the mirror image of invoices and produced in exactly the same way. Probably the most important thing with these is to make sure that they match the original invoice. Have prices changed since it was issued? Did you give a discount?

1 *Check the details of the items in the original invoice.*
2 *Begin as for an invoice, but select* Credit *as the* **Type.** *The* **Format** *should be* Product *or* Service *to match the invoice.*
3 *Enter the details and price of the credited item or service.*
4 *Double-click on the Description to open the Edit Item Line window if you need to edit any of the details.*
5 *Enter any collection or return information on the* **Order Details** *tab.*
6 *Click* **Save.**

6.3 Printing invoices

Whether you are printing one invoice or many, the steps are the same. The difference is in how you start.

▶ *With a single invoice or credit note, it is simplest to print it while you are creating it. Just click the **Print** button on the Invoice window – and note that the invoice is automatically saved when you do this.*

▶ *If you are processing a set of invoices, it is more efficient to start printing from the **Invoicing** window.*

1 *Open the **Invoicing** window.*
2 *Select the invoices and click **Print**.*

A preview of an
invoice report
designed for pre-
printed stationery

3 *The Report Browser window will open and display the available invoice layouts. Pick one.*
4 *Select **Preview** to check the output on screen before printing.*
5 *If the layout works, you can print from the Preview window, or close it and click **Print** in the Invoicing window.*
6 *Close the Report Browser window.*

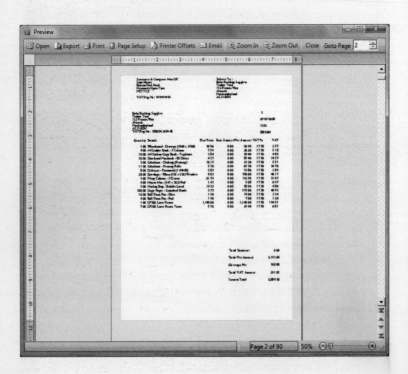

6.4 Updating ledgers

When you create and save an invoice or credit note, its information is stored in your files, but the effect of the transaction on other accounts is not recorded immediately. To 'post' the data to the relevant customers' and nominal accounts, you must use the **Update** button.

The system always shows the transactions it has performed. These can be output to paper or file, if required, or simply viewed on screen.

1 *Select the* **Post Invoices** *task in the Customers module, if necessary, to open the Invoicing window.*
2 *If only certain invoices are to be posted, select them first – otherwise all the unposted invoices will be processed.*
3 *Click* **Update**.
4 *If a paper copy is needed, select* **Printer***; if you need a file copy for future reference select* **File***; otherwise select* **Preview**.
5 *Click* **OK**.

6.5 Batch invoices

Invoices and credit notes for your customers are normally dealt with through the Invoicing window, where they can be created, printed and the transactions posted to the ledgers. There are also batch invoices and credits routines which in the Customer module, are there to record the transactions when invoices or credit notes have been produced manually. In the Supplier module, they are the main way to record your transactions.

1 *In the* **Suppliers** *(or* **Customers***) window click* **Invoice.**
2 *Select the account from the* **A/C** *list.*
3 *Enter the date and other details.*
4 *Enter the* **Net** *amount.*
5 *If the price is VAT-inclusive, click* **Calc Net.**

A/C	Date	Ref	Ex.Ref	N/C	Dept	Project Ref	Details	Net	T/C	VAT
STE001	02/01/2010	AP103		4001	1		Hard drives	242.60	T1	42.46
HAU001	02/01/2010	AP103		4100	6		Tape backu...	632.50		110.69

A/C Hausser GMBH
N/C Sales Export
Tax Rate 17.50
Total 1028.25
875.10   153.15

Save Discard Calc. Net Memorise Recall Close

6 *Repeat steps 2 to 5 as needed.*
7 *Click* **Save***, then* **Close.**

How many lines?
An invoice can be recorded in a single line. If it is for several items and you want to record each separately, use a new line for each, but keep the same Ref code.

5 *Click* **Save** *to return to the* **Invoice** *window, then save the invoice.*

The invoice will be added to the list of recurring items. At the start of each day, Sage 50 will check this list and if any are due to be issued, you will be prompted to deal with them.

6 *In the* **Invoicing** *window, click the* **Recurring** *toolbar button.*

Memorised and Recurring Invoices			
Reference	Description	Recurring?	Suspended?
Compton	Compton repeat invoice	Yes	No
S D Ent	SD Enterprise repeat	Yes	No
WS12	Web site hosting ...	Yes	No

Process | Delete | Edit | Frequency | Print List | Cancel

7 *At the* **Memorised Invoices** *window, click* **Process.**

Process Recurring Entries

Show transactions up to: 04/01/2010

Account	Ref	Date	Description	Amount	Include
COM001	Compton	12/12/2009	Compton rep...	487.80	☑
SDE001	S D Ent	11/12/2009	SD Enterprise rep...	4700.00	☑

Process | Cancel

8 *Tick the* **Include** *box for those invoices that you want to generate and click* **Process.** *You can then update the ledgers and print these as for normal invoices.*

6.7 Order processing

Sage 50 has sales and order processing routines. Invoices are generated automatically from these when the orders are marked as completed. In addition, sales order processing is linked to stock control, allocating items from stock – if available – against the order and updating those records. A delivery note can be generated when the order is completed.

A sales/purchase order is created in almost exactly the same way as an invoice. Here's the process for a sales order:

1 *In the* **Customer** *module, select the* **New Sales Order** *task.*
2 *If* Sales Order *is not the default* **Type**, *select it.*

3 *Set the* **Date.**

4 *Select the* **A/C** *code from the list.*

5 *Select the Product* **Code** *or select S1, S2 or S3. If necessary enter or edit the description.*

6 *Enter the* **Quantity.** *The* **Net** *will then be calculated.*

7 *Repeat steps 5 and 6 for each item.*

8 *If the order is not yet complete, click* **Save.** *When the goods are ready for despatch, reopen the order and come back to this point.*

9 *If the order is complete, click* **Complete.**

10 *At the* **Confirm** *dialog box, click* **Yes** *if you want to create the invoice and delivery note, and update the stock. Click* **No** *to just create the delivery note. This can be printed immediately or left on file for later printing.*

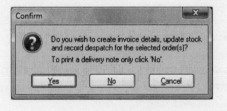

Labels

If you want address labels to send out the invoices, there are ready-made layouts available. Click the Labels toolbar button to start. (See page 124 for more on labels.)

THINGS TO REMEMBER

▶ *Invoices and credit notes can be produced through the Invoicing window.*

▶ *When creating product invoices, prices are taken from the relevant product records. The details of each product can be adjusted, as necessary.*

▶ *With service invoices, a job can be broken down into several items, each of which can be described over several lines.*

▶ *Credit notes are produced in the same way as invoices. The notes' reference numbers should match those of the original invoice.*

▶ *Each invoice can be printed as it is created, or a selected batch can be printed in one operation later.*

▶ *Transactions are not recorded in the relevant accounts until the Update ledgers routine is run.*

▶ *You can create recurring invoices where customers take the same items or service regularly.*

7

Credit control

In this chapter you will learn:
- *about managing customer credit*
- *about day sales analysis*
- *how to record contacts in Sage 50*
- *about aged analysis and write-offs of debts*

7.1 Managing customer credit

Good control of your cash flows – in and out of the business –
is an essential part of successful management. And to keep control
of those flows, you need to be able to find out quickly and easily
how much money is owing, for how long, and to and from whom.
Sage 50's credit control facilities can give you that information.

The key one for inward flows is the **Customer Credit Control**
window.

1 *Go to the* **Customer** *module and from the* **Tasks** *list select*
    Chase Debt.
2 *In the* **Show** *field, at the top of the window, select*
    Outstanding, Overdue, *or* **Promised,** *or other category, to filter
    the display.*

SORTING

The list can be sorted in order of any column by clicking on the column header; e.g. to sort in ascending order of the amount owing:

▶ Click once on the Balance header.

To sort into descending order:

▶ Click on the header a second time.

CREDIT CONTROL TOOLS

The Chase debt window has a large set of buttons in its toolbar. Seven of these can be covered briefly:

▶ **Record** *displays the customer's record.*
▶ **Activity** *displays the trading Activity tab of the selected customer – you can only select one at a time in this window.*
▶ **Dispute** *is used to record a dispute on a transaction.*
▶ **Charges** *runs a wizard to apply charges on overdue accounts. To be able to do this, you need to set up finance rates in the*

Terms tab *of the Configuration Editor, and turn on Can Charge Credit on your customer records – and agree the terms with your customers!*

▶ **Letters** *and* **Statement** *both open the Report Browser to create and print appropriate letters or statements for the selected customer(s).*

▶ **Reports** *opens the Report Browser and offers a wide range of reports to help you manage your credit customers.*

Let's have a closer look at the facilities offered through the other five buttons.

7.2 Day Sales Analysis

The analysis window shows you how much is outstanding and overdue. You can see this as a graph, if you want an overview of how the business is doing, or in detail.

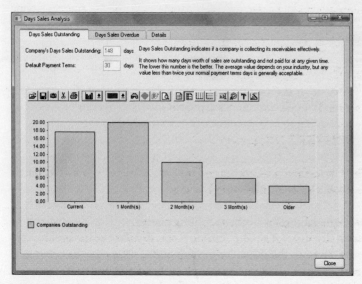

The graphs give you an overview of the payment patterns.

1 *Click* **Analysis** *to open the* **Days Sales Analysis** *window.*
2 *Switch to the* **Days Sales Outstanding** *or* **Overdue** *tabs to see the graphs.*
3 *Use the* **Details** *tab to see exactly how much is owing and for how long.*

A/C.	Name	Receivables Outstanding	Receivables Overdue	ys Sales Outstanding	Days Sales Overdue
A1D001	A1 Design Services	0.00	0.00	0	0
ABS001	ABS Garages Ltd	2533.31	2533.31	33	33
BBS001	Bobs Building Supplies	0.00	0.00	0	0
BRI001	Fred Briant	0.00	0.00	0	0
BRO001	Bronson Inc	0.00	0.00	0	0
BUS001	Business Exhibitions	2066.62	2066.62	47	47
CASH001	Cash and Credit Card ..	0.00	0.00	0	0
CGS001	County Golf Supplies	2028.03	2028.03	41	41
COM001	Compton Packaging	2807.04	2807.04	31	31
DATARECO	Data Recovery Ltd	0.00	0.00	0	0
DST001	Johnson Design & Bui..	0.00	0.00	0	0
FGL001	F G Landscape & De ..	11260.26	11260.26	57	57
GRA001	Graham Electonics	4149.09	3895.53	37	36
HAU001	Hausser GMBH	1975.16	1975.16	37	37
JSS001	John Smith Studios	972.07	972.07	48	48
KIN001	Kingham & French	7398.35	7398.35	87	87

Average Company's Days Sales Outstanding: 48 days   Default Payment Terms: 30 days
Average Company's Days Sales Overdue: 17 days

4 *Click on the headings to sort by the amount or the length of time that the invoices have been owing. This can be useful in deciding where to concentrate your efforts.*

7.3 Communications

Anyone who runs a business dealing mainly with credit customers – especially if it is a smaller business and the customers are larger firms – knows the difficulty of finding the right balance between prompting the slower payers with sufficient vigour to be taken seriously and harrassing them to the point where you lose future custom. Life is simpler in those countries which have strict limits on how quickly debts must be paid!

The Communications routine allows you to keep a track on when a customer was contacted, and what was agreed.

1 *Select the customer.*
2 *Click **Communications** to open the customer's record at the communications tab. This shows any contacts made to date.*

3 *Click **New** to record a new contact.*
4 *In the **Contact Details** section, select **Telephone**, **Letter/Fax/ e-Mail** or **Meeting**. The details will vary according to the nature of the contact, and for telephone calls the Timer display will appear, so that you can time its duration.*
5 *Fill in the details, and the outcome or results.*
6 *Click **Save** to store the details and return to the Communications display.*

7.4 Cash Flow

The Cash Flow window shows the state of the bank account(s)
if payments are made and received on their forecast dates.
When using this, it is important to remember that it is based on
guesswork – when figures are shown to the exact penny it is all too
easy to think that they are exact.

1 *Click the* **Cash Flow** *button to open the* **Cash Flow** *window.*
2 *In the* **Bank Accounts** *area at the top right, tick the
   checkboxes for those accounts that you want to include in the
   running balance.*
3 *To change a forecast date, click on the calendar icon and
   set the date.*
4 *Tick the* **Inc?** *checkbox to include the receipt or payment in
   the running balance – or clear the checkbox if you decide that
   the money will not come in or go out on that day.*
5 *After making any changes, click* **Refresh** *to update the screen
   display.*

The **Send To...** *button will export the data to Excel if you want
to process it further.*

7.5 Aged analysis

The Aged Analysis window shows the amounts owing by the selected customers (or to the selected suppliers) in each ageing period.

The analysis can be started from the Credit Control window or from the toolbars in the Customer or Supplier windows. Use the latter approach if you want to examine a number of accounts at the same time.

1 *In the* **Chase Debt** *window, select the accounts and click* **Aged.**

2 *Set the report date and the date to include payments to, and click* **OK.**

3 *The* **Aged Balances** *window will open, showing summary information for the selected account(s). Note the totals at the bottom – you can see these as a graph on the* **Graph** *tab.*

Aged Balances as of 3rd September 2008

A/C	YTD	Credit Limit	Balance	Future	Current	1 Month(s)	2 Month(s)	3 Month(s)	Older
BUS001	4959.81	4000.00	2066.62						2066.62
CASH001	30561.30	0.00							
CGS001	3922.44	3000.00	2028.03						2028.03
COM001	4452.08	4000.00	2807.04			975.60		487.80	1343.64
DATARECO	0.00	2500.00		5274.23					
DST001	3947.99	2000.00							
FGL001	10867.60	5000.00	11260.26						11260.26
GRA001	4846.01	4000.00	4149.09	-253.56					4149.09
HAU001	2295.85	4000.00	1975.16	632.50					1975.16
JSS001	3001.20	1000.00	972.07						972.07
KIN001	16062.58	6000.00	7398.35						7398.35
MAC001	10592.14	4000.00	6927.16						6927.16
MIB001	3059.60	1000.00	3597.16						3597.16
MIL001	10562.52	2000.00	2307.84						2307.84
MOR001	1490.88	4000.00	392.67						392.67
PAT001	2412.51	1000.00	915.24						915.24

Future	Current	1 Month(s)	2 Month(s)	3 Month(s)	Older	Balance	Debtors
10633.79	0.00	5675.60	4700.00	487.80	77670.37	88633.77	94997.21

[Detailed] [Print List] [Close]

4 For a closer look at an account, double-click on it to display it in the **Detailed Aged Analysis** *window*.

Detailed Aged Analysis

MAC001 Macolm Hall Associates | Graph

No	Type	Future	Current	1 Month(s)	2 Month(s)	3 Month(s)	Older	Ref	Date
767	SI						3319.95	47	20/03/200
995	SI						3607.21	56	14/04/200

Current	1 Month(s)	2 Month(s)	3 Month(s)	Older
0.00	0.00	0.00	0.00	6927.16

[Close]

7.6 Write offs

Write offs, refunds and returns are all handled by a wizard that is started from the **Write off** button in the Credit Control window.

Here's how low value write offs are managed – the other types and refunds and returns are similarly straightforward.

1 *In the* **Chase Debt** *window, click* **Write off.**
2 *At the Write Off, Refunds and Returns Wizard, select Write off Customer Transactions below a value. Click* **Next.**

Write Off, Refunds and Returns Wizard

Write Off, Refund and Returns

Select the area in which to make the required amendments.

Area
Refund Credit Notes
Payment on Account Refund
Write off Customer Accounts
Write off Customer Transactions
Write off Customer Transactions below a value
Write off Customer Small Overpayments

Cancel   Help   Back   Next   Finish

3 *Enter the maxim value to write off. Click* **Next.**

Write Off, Refunds and Returns Wizard

Write Off, Refund and Returns

Enter the value below which a transaction will be written off -

200.00

Cancel   Help   Back   Next   Finish

4 *Any transactions below the limit will be listed. Make sure that only those that you really want to write off are selected.*

Write Off, Refunds and Returns Wizard

Write Off, Refund and Returns

Select the outstanding invoice transaction(s) from the list below that are to be written off then click on "Next" to continue, if you have entered the wrong amount click on the "Back" button to change the amount

No	A/C	N/C	Date	Invoice	Details	d	Amount
383	COM001	4000	02/02/2009	18	Whiteboar...		183.2
1242	BRO001	4000	02/01/2009	86	Calculato...		103.5

[Swap]   [Clear]

[Cancel] [Help]   [Back] [Next] [Finish]

---

5 *Set the date and add a reference for the operation.*

Write Off, Refunds and Returns Wizard

Write Off, Refund and Returns

Please select the date that you wish to use for the transactions you have selected and enter an Additional Reference if required.

Date   03/11/2009

Additional Reference   write offs under £200

[Cancel] [Help]   [Back] [Next] [Finish]

VAT cash accounting?

Note that the use of the Write off, Refunds and Returns
Wizard is not recommend where the firm uses VAT cash
accounting as the transactions are posted with a tax code that
would exclude them from the VAT return.

7.7 Managing supplier credit

The credit control window looks almost the same when opened
from the Suppliers area, though it is now called Manage Payments.
There is a slightly different set of toolbar buttons here, of course,
including this new one – **Suggest Payment.** If you want to pay
several suppliers at the same time, it is simpler to use this routine
than the Pay Supplier routine in the Bank module (see page 167).

1 *Go to the Supplier module and select the* **Manage Payments**
   task.
2 *Click the* **Suggest Payment** *tool to open the Suggested
   Payments window.*

A/C	Name	Overdue	Outstanding	Credit Limit	On Hold	Priority	Payment Amount	Reason
SUP001	Superior Technologies Ltd	8848.88	8848.88	15000.00			8848.88	
WIS002	Wiseman Paper Products	5868.13	5868.13	10000.00			2500.00	
SUP002	Superclean	1762.50	1762.50	3000.00			1762.50	
CON001	Concept Stationery Supplies	1644.39	1644.39	17000.00				
MCN001	McNally Computer Supplies	484.64	484.64	10000.00				
SDE001	S D Enterprises	352.50	352.50	5000.00				
THO001	Thompsons Electricals	337.11	337.11	4000.00				
UNI001	Unique Systems	150.40	640.76	5000.00				
WIS001	Wise Electricals Ltd	82.28	82.28	14000.00				
QUA001	Quality Motors	30.22	30.22	20000.00			0.00	

Available Funds: Funds for Payment 15000.00 / Paid 0.00 / Remaining 15000.00 / Still to Pay 19561.05

Bank Account: Bank A/C 1200 Bank Current Account / Balance -40486.24 / Min Limit -120000.00

The funds remaining are less than the amount still to pay.

Suggest | Make Payment... | Clear | Print List | Close

3 *Decide how much money you have available and enter this in
   the* **Funds for Payment** *field at the top left. You can allocate
   funds to suppliers in two ways.*

Either:

4 Click **Suggest**. *The funds will be allocated from the top down – paying each supplier in full, as far as possible then allocating a partial payment with any remaining cash.*

or

5 *Allocate the funds by typing in values or using the calculator – the latter being very handy if you want to work out how much is left after earlier allocations. Note that the system does not work this out for you. The* **Paid** *and* **Remaining** *values are only updated after you have made the payment – not simply allocated an amount.*

6 *When you have worked out how much to pay each, click* **Make Payment....**

7 *The* **Supplier Payment** *window will open, showing the outstanding transactions. You can pay all or a selection of these.*

8 *To pay a selected transaction, click on it and enter the amount to pay or click* **Pay in Full** *to pay the total amount.*

9 *To pay all transactions fully, click* **Automatic**. *Note that if insufficent funds were allocated to this supplier at the earlier stage, the transactions will be paid from the top down until nothing is let.*

10 *Click* **Save** *to record the payments in your files, then select the next supplier from the drop down* **Payee** *list, or click* **Close** *to return to the* **Suggested Payments** *window.*

Cheque printing

Sage 50 can print your cheques for you – see page 172.

THINGS TO REMEMBER

▶ *The credit control facilities will show you clearly who owes you money, how much and for how long.*

▶ *Keeping records of your contacts with customers is an essential part of good credit control management.*

▶ *The Cash Flow window can help to predict the state of your bank account, if used thoughtfully.*

▶ *The aged analysis facility will show what bills are overdue and by how long.*

▶ *There's a wizard to help you manage write-offs, refunds and returns.*

▶ *The routines for managing supplier credit includes one for allocating funds against several invoices in one batch.*

8

The Bank tasks

In this chapter you will learn:

- *about the Bank tasks and tools*
- *about reconciliation*
- *how to record payments made and received*
- *how to print cheques and remittance advice slips*

8.1 The Bank module

This module gives you a different view of, and more ways of working with, those Nominal accounts which are used for the payment and receipt of money. The routines here can be used to make and record payments to suppliers, record receipts from customers, set up recurring payments, move money between accounts, reconcile your accounts with the bank statements and similar activities.

Note that in the Bank List, you can only select one account at a time – and for some operations, you don't need to select any.

To examine a Bank account:

1 *Select an account.*
2 *Click* **Record.**
3 *Go to the* **Bank Details** *and* **Contact** *tabs to see or update contact information for the bank.*

This window has so many toolbar buttons that they may well not all be displayed on your screen. If there is a double chevron at the right end of the toolbar, click this to reach the overflow.

4 Go to the **Activity** tab to examine transactions that have passed through that account.

5 Click **Show Details** *if you want to see the details of any transaction, e.g. to see which invoices are covered by a sales receipt. The main display area will shrink up to make room for a details pane beneath.*

6 Click **Show** *if you want to view only those transactions from a given month, or the reconciled or unreconciled ones, or to define a Custom Range – you can set the range of numbers, and/or the type to display, and/or the date range.*

Activity Range | X

Transaction Range

From: `1`

To: `1275`

Transaction Type

Type to Display: `SR - Sales Receipts`

Outstanding Transactions Only? ☐

Date Range

From: `01/11/2009`

To: `31/12/2009`

[OK] [Cancel]

The initial date range is from 01/01/1980 to 31/12/2099! Clearly your records won't cover that range, and it is a fiddly job resetting the calendar to more realistic limits.

Bank accounts in the Nominal module

The Bank accounts can also be opened through the Nominal module, and you must use this to reach the graphs and the budgeting facilities.

8.2 Reconciliation

Reconciliation is one of those chores that cannot be automated fully, but at least the Sage 50 system makes it straightforward. As you mark items that match entries in your bank statement, the system calculates and displays the difference between your recorded end balance and that of the bank statement. If they do not match after you have worked through the list, you can see how much it is adrift and will probably have a clear idea of the source of the problem.

1 *Select an account.*
2 *Click* **Reconcile** *on the Bank Accounts toolbar.*
3 *At the* **Statement Summary** *dialog box, enter the* **Ending Balance** *from your bank statement – the balance in your Sage 50 Bank account will have been written in as the default.*
4 *If the statement shows interest earned or bank charges, enter the amounts and select the appropriate N/C codes.*

Statement Summary			X
Bank	1200	Bank Current Account	
Statement Reference :		WGR Nov 09	
Ending Balance :	9243.96	Statement Date :	04/11/2009
Interest Earned :			
Amount :	0.00	Date : 04/11/2009	NC :
Account Charges :			
Amount :	156.70	Date : 04/11/2009	NC : 7901
	OK	Cancel	

5 *Click* **OK** *to open the* **Bank Reconciliation** *window.*

Date	No.	Reference	Details	Payments	Receipts	
20/10/2009	1252	DD/STO	Rent Direct Debit	1200.00		
28/10/2009	1253	DD/STO	Hire Purchase Payment	150.00		
28/10/2009	1254	DD/STO	Hire Purchase Interest	5.55		
28/10/2009	1256	DD/STO	Hire Purchase Interest	5.55		
03/11/2009	1262	(BACS)	Purchase Payment	22000.00		
03/11/2009	1263		Purchase Payment	1762.50		
03/11/2009	1264		Purchase Payment	8848.88		

Statement — Edit... Reference WGR Nov 09 End Date 04/11/2009 End Balance: 9243.96

Find... | Swap | Clear | 0.00 | Match >>

Date	No.	Reference	Details	Payments	Receipts	Balance	
02/11/2009	1257		Purchase Payment	4292.05		2900.35	
02/11/2009	1259		Purchase Payment	316.07		2584.28	
02/11/2009	1260	EXP	Accom.	846.00		1738.28	
02/11/2009	1261	4543	Sales Receipt		3539.02	5277.30	
03/11/2009	1265		Sales Receipt		4186.62	9463.92	
03/11/2009	1266	DD/STO	Electricty Direct Debit	162.00		9301.92	
03/11/2009	1267	DD/STO	Hire Purchase Payment	150.00		9151.92	

<< Unmatch | 0.00 | Swap | Clear | Adjust...

Book Balance	Totals Payments:	Receipts:	Matched Balance	– Statement Balance	= Difference
-55267.97	17575.12	33239.00	9151.92	9243.96	-92.04

Reconcile | Save | Print... | Send to Excel.. | View History | Close

6 *Work through the list. Select an unmatched item in the top list. If you can match it with the bank statement, mark it off on the statement and click* **Match** *to move it to the Matched list below.*

7 *If you do not have the time or the information to complete the reconciliation, you can click* **Save** *to save the work done so far, then restart the process later using the saved data.*

8 *When all the items have been reconciled, if the* **Difference** *is not 0.00, you need to track down the missing transactions, or identify the ones entered incorrectly. When you have found them, click* **Adjust** *and enter the details.*

9 *When you are done, click* **Reconcile**.

10 *If there is a difference between your Bank account and the statement amount, you can add an adjustment at this point, or choose to ignore the difference.*

Adjustment

Details

Nominal Code	Date	Reference	Department
2204	04/11/2009	ADJ	0

Details

Adjustment Posting

Tax Code	Payment	Receipt
T9 0.00	92.04	0.00

Save   Discard   Close

8.3 Payments and receipts

There are five routines here. New Payments and New Receipts are designed to handle cash transactions – and these can be done in batches if required. The Pay Supplier and Receive Payment are there to record settlement of credit transactions. (These can also be accessed through the Customer and Supplier modules.) Finally, the Batch routine offers a convenient way to deal with payments for credit purchases, in batches.

The example here is from the **New Payment** routine, but the same method is used to process cash receipts.

1 *Select a Bank account.*
2 *Click* **Payment** *or select the* **New Payment** *task.*
3 *Set the* **Date** *and give a* **Ref** *code if required.*
4 *Select the* **N/C** *code of the account for the goods or service.*
5 *Enter the* **Details** *of the sale or purchase.*
6 *Enter the amount into the* **Net** *box – if this is VAT-inclusive, click* **Calc Net** *to split it into Net and VAT.*

7 *If you want to use the cheque printing facilities, click* **Print Cheque.**

8 *Select the Payee from the suppliers list, or type in the name and address, then click* **Save.** *The details will be added to the cheque list for later printing (see page 172).*

9 *Repeat for any other items.*
10 *Click* **Save** *and then* **Close.**

8.4 Receive Payment

Use this routine for recording monies received from credit customers, one at a time. The Receive Payment window shows the outstanding invoices for the selected customer. Receipts can be either allocated to specific invoices, or automatically set against invoices in reference number (not *date*) order.

1   *Select the Bank account to take the money.*
2   *Click* **Customer** *or select the* **Receive Payment** *task.*

3   *Select the customer from the A/C list.*
4   *Set the* **Date** *and enter the* **Ref.**
5   *Enter the* **Amount** *of the payment.*
6   *Click* **Automatic** *to set this against invoices. The monies will be allocated from the top down until the amount is exhausted, paying each in full, and the last one whatever is left.*

or

7   *Select an invoice and enter an amount or click* **Pay in Full.** *If there is a discount, enter this in the end column. Repeat as required.*
8   *Click* **Save.**
9   *Go back to step 3 for the next customer, or click* **Close.**

8.5 Supplier payments

The Receive Payment and Pay Supplier routines are virtually identical in the way that they work, though they look a little different as the Pay Supplier window has a cheque display at the top.

As you enter amounts against invoices, the system calculates the total and shows it in words and figures in the 'cheque' at the top.

1 *Select the account from which the payment will be made.*
2 *Click* **Supplier**.
3 *Set the* **Date** *and enter the* **Cheque No.**, *or leave this at BACS.*
4 *Select the supplier from the* **Payee** *drop-down list.*

Either
5 *Enter the amount on the cheque and click* **Automatic** *to allocate this to invoices.*
or
6 *Select an invoice and enter an amount or click* **Pay in Full**. *This will be added to the total amount in the cheque display at the top.*

or

7 *If there is a discount, enter the full* **Payment**, *then the* **Discount** – *it will be deducted from the payment.*

8 *Click* **Save**. *If a cheque is required, the details will be added to the cheque list (see page 172).*

9 *Go back to step 3 for the next payment, or click* **Close**.

8.6 Batch payments

In the last chapter we met the Suggested Payments routine that could be run from the Manage Payments window. Here is an alternative way to keep on top of your debts.

The Batch Purchase Payments window lists all the outstanding invoices – rather than the total owing to each supplier. While this does mean that you could be faced with a long list, it also enables you to pay invoices selectively if there have been any disputes over delivery, quality or prices.

The routine can only be started from the toolbar button, or from the context menu that appears when you right-click on the Bank Accounts window.

1 *Select the Bank account from which payments are to be made.*

2 *Click* **Batch** *or right-click on the account and select* **Batch...** *from the menu.*

3 *If you want to pay all the invoices fully, click* **Pay All**. *(And if when you see the* **Total** *figure you decide that this is a mistake, click* **Discard** *to clear all payments back to 0.00.)*

4 *Locate the invoices that you want to pay and either type in the amount or click* **Pay in Full**.

5 *If there is a discount, enter the* **Payment**, *then the* **Discount**.

6 *Repeat 4 and 5 as required, then click* **Save** *and* **Close**.

Changing accounts

In all the other receipts and payments routines it is possible
to select a different Bank account from within the routine.
You cannot do this here, so do make sure you have the right
account when you start.

8.7 Recurring entries

Direct debits, standing orders and other regular payments to
suppliers or from customers can be set up as recurring entries and
processed automatically.

There are two ways to view recurring entries and three ways to
start adding a new one. They all do the same job!

To add a recurring entry:
1 *Click* **Recurring** – *this will open the* **Recurring Entries**
   window.

Type	Ref	Details	Amount Posting Frequency	Next Posting	Postings Made Postings Remaining	Posted Value Remaining Value
BP	DD/STO	Electricity Direct Debit	162.00 4 Month(s)	01/12/2009	3 Perpetual	0.00 Perpetual
BP	DD/STO	Hire Purchase Interest	5.55 1 Month(s)	28/11/2009	12 36	0.00 199.80
BP	DD/STO	Hire Purchase Payment	150.00 1 Month(s)	28/11/2009	12 36	0.00 5400.00
BP	DD/STO	Loan Repayment	150.00 0 Day(s)	Suspended	0 Perpetual	0.00 Perpetual

Add   Edit   Delete   Process   Print List   Activity   Close

2 *Click to open the* **Add/Edit Recurring Entry** *dialog box.*
(This can also be opened from the **New Recurring Transaction**
task in the Bank window.)

Add / Edit Recurring Entry

Transaction Type	Bank/Cash/Credit Card Payment

Recurring Entry From / To

Bank A/C	1200	Bank: Current Account
Nominal Code	7102	Water Rates

Recurring Entry Details

Transaction Ref	DD/STO
Transaction Details	Water charges direct debit
Department	0

Posting Frequency

Every	1 Month(s)	Total Required Postings	10
Start Date	14/01/2010	Finish Date	14/10/2010
Next Posting Date	14/01/2010	Suspend Posting ?	☐
Last Posted			

Posting Amounts

Net Amount	85.25	Tax Code	T1 17.50	VAT	14.92

OK   Cancel

3   *Select the* **Type** *of transaction – it can be Payment, Receipt, Transfer (between bank accounts), on account payment from customer, or journal debit or credit. Remember that every journal entry must have a matching debit or credit entry, and you must create these yourself.*

4   *Select the* **Bank A/C** *and* **Nominal Code** *that the payment is made from and to.*

5   *Enter the* **Details** *to identify the transaction.*

6   *Set the frequency, number of payments and date of the first one – leave the* **Total Required Postings** *at 0 if this payment is to be made regularly for the indefinite future.*

7   *Enter the* **Net Amount**, *and the tax if appropriate.*

8   *Click* **OK** *to return to the Recurring Entries window.*

To view or post entries:

1   *Open the* **Recurring Entries** *window*

2   *To change an entry, select it and click* **Edit.**

3   *If the entries are all correct, click* **Process** *to start posting the transactions.*

4   *At the* **Process Recurring Entries** *window, set the date up to which you want to show transactions.*

5   *If required, you can edit the* **Due Date**, **Net** *and* **Tax** *fields.*

6   *When you are happy that the entries are correct, click* **Post.**

	Type	Account	Nominal	Due Date	Frequency	Ref	Dept	Details	Net	T/C	Tax
	BP	1200	7200	01/11/2009	4 Month(s)	DD/STO	0	Electricity Direct D...	150.00	T3	12.00
	BP	1200	2310	28/10/2009	1 Month(s)	DD/STO	0	Hire Purchase Pay...	150.00	T9	0.00
	BP	1200	7903		1 Month(s)	DD/STO	0	Hire Purchase Inte...	5.55	T9	0.00

▶ *Now go and write the cheques. This routine does not do that for you – all it does is record the transactions.*

8.8 Cheque printing

Sage 50 has a neat facility to print the cheques that can arise from the payments routines.

▶ With **Make Payments**, *in the Suppliers module, a cheque request is generated automatically, unless the supplier has been set for BACS payment.*
▶ With **Payments** *in the Bank module, a cheque request is generated if you click the **Print Cheques** button.*

There are six ready-made layouts for printing cheques, with or without remittance slips, on pre-printed 12 inch or A4 paper. If none of these does the job, you can edit them or create your own print layouts in Report Designer.

1 *In the Bank module, click **Cheques** on the toolbar.*
2 *At the **Print Cheques** window, select the cheques you want to print – or leave them unselected to print them all.*

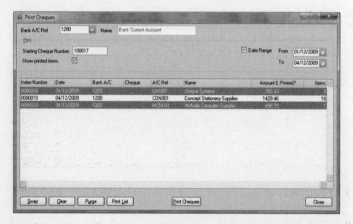

3 *Make sure that the* **Starting Cheque Number** *is correct.*
4 *Click* **Print Cheques.**

5 *Select a layout and the output – and remember that if you pick*
Preview, *you can carry on and print from here.*
6 *Click* **Run.**

7 *The printout will be generated, and you will be asked if the*
cheques printed OK.
8 *Click* **Yes** *to assign cheque numbers to the transactions and*
to mark them as printed in the cheque list.

A cheque and remittance printout, designed for pre-printed stationery, seen in preview. Note that at some Zoom levels, the preview layout can go askew – if it looks wrong, set the Zoom to 100% and check again.

Remittance advice slips

If payment is by BACS, or cheques are printed without remittance advice, or cheques are handwritten, you can print remittance advice slips separately. Click **Remittance** in the Bank module to open the Print Bank Remittances window. This lists all recent payments – select the ones for which you want advice slips.

4 *In the* **Frequency** *area, set it to* **Every** *so many days/months or years, and give a* **Start Date**. *If only a limited number of invoices are to be issued, e.g. as for an annual contract, then set the* **Total Required**, *otherwise leave this at zero for indefinite repetiton.*

CALCULATING VAT

The system calculates VAT, whether prices are given Net or VAT-inclusive. Prices are always entered into the Net column.

▶ *With Net prices, the VAT will appear automatically when you click into the T/C column or into the line below.*
▶ *With VAT-inclusive prices, click Calc Net and the system will split the total into the Net and VAT elements.*

CREDIT NOTES

These are handled in almost exactly the same way as invoices. The key point to note is that the reference number here must be that of the invoice against which the credit is being given.

1 *Look up the Reference number of the invoice in the customer or supplier's Activity tab.*
2 *Click Credit in the main Customers (or Suppliers) window.*
3 *Complete as for invoices, but with the original Ref numbers.*

6.6 Recurring invoices

If you are issuing an invoice regularly to a customer, e.g. for rent, a maintenance contract or a standing order for goods, then this can be automated by setting it up as a recurring invoice. It only takes a moment to do, but it saves you having to generate a new invoice each time – and it helps to ensure that invoices are produced on time.

1 *Start as you would with any invoice, filling in all relevant details.*
2 *When you have finished, return to the Details tab, and click the Memorise button in the bottom row.*
3 *At the Memorise dialog box, type a reference and description to identify it in the recurring entries list.*

8.9 Transfers

The Transfer routine is used to record the movement of monies between Bank accounts, e.g. restocking petty cash, paying the credit card bill, or transferring cash between your current and deposit accounts at the bank.

1 *Click* **Transfer** *or select* **Record Transfer** *from the Tasks.*

2 *Select the* **Account from** *which to transfer.*
3 *Select the* **Account to** *which the money will be transferred.*
4 *Edit the* **Description** *if 'Bank Transfer' does not say enough for you.*
5 *Enter the* **Payment Value.**
6 *Set the* **Date.**
7 *Click* **Save.**
8 *Repeat from step 2 if there are any more transfers, otherwise click* **Close.**

Use the wizard?

The Wizard button here collects the same information, but in a series of steps rather than filling in the form. A less confident operator might find it useful.

8.10 Statements

The Statement button can produce a list of the reconciled transactions, in numerical order and the running balance for all those accounts that have seen activity in the current audit trail. You can output statements for selected accounts only.

The process is kind of backwards – you tell it to run first, then define how to do it! Still, the result is the same.

1 *Click the* **Statement** *tool.*

2 *Select the* **Output** *mode and click* **Run**.

3 *At the* **Criteria** *dialog box, set the range by* **Date** *if required, then click* **OK**.

The Bank module window showing a Bank Statement preview:

Date: 05/01/2010
Time: 11:09:25

Bank Statement

Page: 1

1200
Bank Current Account
Currency: Pound Sterling

Bank Balance: £   1905.95

Bridge Computers
11 The High Street
Oldbridge
Midshire
OB1 2ER

Date From: 26/10/2009
Date To: 04/11/2009

No	Date	Ref	Details	Payments £	Receipts £	Balance £
			B/Fwd Balance			-6,217.05
1104	27/10/2009		Sales Receipt		1,173.07	-5,043.98
1107	27/10/2009		Sales Receipt		12,244.52	7,200.54
1121	27/10/2009	4543	Sales Receipt		3,539.02	10,739.56
1122	28/10/2009		Sales Receipt		4,186.62	14,926.18
1124	28/10/2009	986	Sales Receipt		2,079.34	17,005.52
1127	28/10/2009		Purchase Payment	4,292.05		12,713.47
1172	28/10/2009	EXP	Accom.	346.00		11,867.47
1220	28/10/2009	DD/STO	Hire Purchase Payment	150.00		11,717.47
1260	03/11/2009		Purchase Payment	316.07		11,401.40
1261	03/11/2009	(BACS)	Purchase Payment	2,249.48		9,151.92

8.11 Reports

The Bank module offers over 40 summary and detailed reports,
reflecting the accounts and transaction routines of the Bank
module. The layouts are all fixed, but you control the content by
setting the range of dates and reference numbers, and by selecting
the Nominal and Bank accounts to include.

There are 15 sets of ready-made reports:

▸ *Three varieties of Bank payments and receipts: together and
  separate, detailed and summary.*
▸ *Cash payments and cash receipts: detailed and summary.*
▸ *Credit card payments and receipts: detailed and summary.*

- ▶ *Customer reports: detailed and summary, in all or just the cash sales.*
- ▶ *Purchase and bank payments: as a single report.*
- ▶ *Reconciled transactions: sorted in different ways.*
- ▶ *Reconciled and unreconciled transactions: and non-reconciled or purely unreconciled.*
- ▶ *Unreconciled transactions: either bank report, payments or receipts.*
- ▶ *Sales and Bank receipts: shown together.*
- ▶ *Supplier reports: detailed and summary.*

And, of course, you can create your own reports, or edit any of these, using Report Designer (see Chapter 4).

Most reports can list all the accounts or those in a selected range. Depending upon the type of report, this can be based on the nominal code, date, transaction number or department.

1 *Click the* **Reports** *toolbar button.*
2 *Select a set, and then a layout.*
3 *Choose the output – Printer, Preview, File or E-mail.*

4 *In the* **Criteria** *dialog box, you can specify a range of nominal codes, transaction dates or numbers.*

5 *If you want to check that the criteria select the right things, set a number to preview, instead of running the full report.*

Criteria				

Criteria Values

Enter the values to use for the criteria in this report

| Transaction Date | Between (inclusive) ▾ | 01/12/2009 ▾ | and | 31/12/2009 ▾ |
| Transaction No | Between (inclusive) ▾ | 1 ▴▾ | and | 99999999 ▴▾ |

Preview a sample report for a specified number of records or transactions (0 for all) 0 ▴▾

| Help | | | OK | Cancel |

6 *Click* **OK** *to generate the report.*

THINGS TO REMEMBER

▶ *Use the Bank module to view those Nominal accounts relating to bank, credit card and other money accounts, and to record the movement of money to, from and between them.*

▶ *The Bank accounts should be reconciled with the statements from the bank at regular intervals.*

▶ *Use the bank payments and receipts routines to record cash transactions.*

▶ *Use customer receipts to record money received from credit customers.*

▶ *Payments to your credit suppliers should be recorded through the supplier payments routine.*

▶ *Recurring payments can be set up and processed from this module.*

▶ *Sage 50 can print the cheques that can arise from the payments routines.*

▶ *The Statements routine produces lists of transactions through Bank accounts.*

▶ *Many different Reports are available in the Bank module.*

9

Financial control

In this chapter you will learn:
- *about the audit trail and how to clear it*
- *about the trial balance, profit and loss account and balance sheet*
- *about period end routines*

9.1 Financials

The Financials module gives one-stop access to the key financial tools and reports – the audit trail, month end and year end routines, trial balance, profit and loss account, balance sheet and VAT return, amongst others. Most of these can be accessed through toolbar buttons; the rest through the Tasks list.

1 *Click* Modules *in the Menu bar.*
2 *Select* Financials *from the menu.*

The Financials window will open, showing a list of all current transactions, and with a special set of buttons in the toolbar.

9.2 The Audit Trail

The Audit Trail is a key tool for monitoring and analysing your accounts. It is the record of those transactions that have not yet been fully processed, and those that have been processed but not yet cleared from the system.

The Audit Trail can be viewed, in summary form, in the Financials window. It can be printed out in the same form, or in briefer or more detailed forms through the **Audit** button. The printout routines also allow you to select the range of transactions by date, number, customer or supplier reference.

1 *Click* Audit.

2 *Select the level of details.*
3 *Set the* **Output** *mode.*
4 *Click* **Run.**

5 *At the* **Criteria** *dialog box, define the range to display, or leave the settings at the defaults to show all current transactions.*
6 *Click* **OK.**

Part of a detailed audit printout. The landscape mode works better as there is so much information in each line.

Mark a clear trail!

Make sure that you have a full printout of the audit trail before running the clear routine (page 195).

THE TYPE CODES

These codes are used in the Type column:

BP	Bank Payment	**BR**	Bank Receipt
JC	Journal Credit	**JD**	Journal Debit
PC	Purchase Credit	**PI**	Purchase Invoice
PP	Purchase Payment	**SA**	Sale, payment on account
SC	Sale, Credit	**SI**	Sale, Invoice
SR	Sale Receipt		

9.3 The Trial Balance

In a manual system, the main purpose of the Trial Balance is to check that every credit has its matching debit, and vice versa. This is less of an issue in Sage 50 where most of the double-entries are handled for you. However, there are opportunities for human error, and the Trial Balance will tell you if further investigation is needed. It also provides a convenient summary of the nominal ledger accounts.

The Trial Balance is based on the data from the start of the year up to a chosen month – and, apart from the output mode, that is your only option.

    1 *Click* **Trial.**

2 *Set the **Output** mode and click **Run**.*

Criteria

Criteria Values

Enter the values to use for the criteria in this report

| **Period** | To (inclusive) ▼ | 11. November 2008 ▼ |

Preview a sample report for a specified number of records or transactions (0 for all)   0

Help   OK   Cancel

3 *At the **Criteria** dialog box, select the end month. If you just want a small sample to check the output style, enter the number of accounts you want to see. Click **Run**.*

Period Trial Balance - Preview

Open Export Print Page Setup Printer Offsets Email Zoom In Zoom Out Close Goto Page 1

Time: 12:44:34   **Period Trial Balance**

To Period: Month 11, November 2009

N/C	Name	Debit	Credit
0020	Plant and Machinery	50,000.00	
0021	Plant/Machinery Depreciation		3,485.00
0040	Furniture and Fixtures	16,900.00	
0041	Furniture/Fixture Depreciation		93.00
0050	Motor Vehicles	20,300.00	
0051	Motor Vehicles Depreciation		2,091.92
1001	Stock	35,000.00	
1100	Debtors Control Account	90,640.61	
1200	Bank Current Account		55,267.97
1210	Bank Deposit Account	3,510.00	
1220	Building Society Account	507.53	
1230	Petty Cash	1,130.48	
1240	Company Credit Card	9,358.97	
2100	Creditors Control Account		9,325.75
2200	Sales Tax Control Account		22,182.53
2201	Purchase Tax Control Account	12,203.64	
2202	VAT Liability	14,800.35	
2210	P.A.Y.E.		5,396.79
2211	National Insurance		2,006.98
2230	Pension Fund		120.00
2300	Loans		6,895.00
2310	Hire Purchase		6,160.00
3000	Ordinary Shares		96,332.00
4000	Sales North		179,507.53
4001	Sales South		1,230.00
4002	Sales Scotland		8,472.51
4009	Discounts Allowed	50.00	
4900	Miscellaneous Income		60.03
4905	Distribution and Carriage		870.00
5000	Materials Purchased	51,446.48	
5001	Materials Imported	23,733.00	
5002	Miscellaneous Purchases	1,158.53	
5100	Carriage	1.26	
5200	Opening Stock	40,710.00	
5201	Closing Stock		35,000.00
6200	Sales Promotions	50.00	
6201	Advertising	465.00	
6202	Gifts and Samples	115.00	
6203	P.R. (Literature & Brochures)	1,050.00	
7000	Gross Wages	32,472.11	
7006	Employers N.I.	3,327.24	

Page 1 of 2   100%

A Trial Balance, produced using demo data – any real one would have a lot more to it than this. Notice that the Mispostings Account shows a balance: £155.00 has been mis-recorded somewhere along the line. This needs investigating. Open the Mispostings Account in the Company module and look at the Details tab, to see the months in which the balance appeared.

Output for export?

Output to File is worth considering on any of these financial reports. If the data is saved as in .xls format it can be imported into Excel for further analysis, or use CSV (Comma Separated Values) for import into another type of spreadsheet.

9.4 The Profit and Loss account

With the Profit and Loss account, you define the period, allowing you to examine a month or quarter at any point of the year.

You can also select the chart of accounts, if you have set up one or more of your own (see page 87 for more on creating charts of accounts).

1 *Click* P and L *in the toolbar of the* Financials *window.*
2 *Set the* Output *mode and click* Run.
3 *At the* Criteria *dialog box, select the months to include* From *and* To.

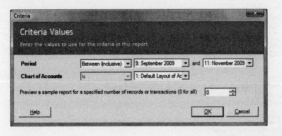

4 *If there are several chart of accounts layouts, select the one to use.*
5 *Click* OK.
6 *If you are outputting to file, the* Save As *dialog box will open. Set the* Save in *folder and* File name *as usual, then drop-down the* Save as type *list and select one of the CSV settings if you want to do further work on the figures, or a PDF, text or Print spool format for printing.*

7 *Click* **Save.**

A sample profit and loss display.

9.5 The Balance Sheet

The Balance Sheet – and the Budget and Prior Year outputs – have the same options as the Profit and Loss account. And as with that, output to file for further analysis, is a common choice

1 *Click* **Balance.**
2 *Set the* **Output** *mode and click* **Run.**
3 *If saving to file, give it a name, select the format and click* **Save.**

4 *At the* **Criteria** *dialog box, select the months to include* **From** *and* **To.**

5 *If there are several chart of accounts layouts, select the one to use.*

6 *Click* **OK.**

A Balance Sheet seen in Preview mode.

9.6 Verification

The verification routines can be used to check your data before you run the VAT Return. There are four possible routines.

1 *Click* **Verify.**

2 *At the* **Verify System** *dialog box, select the type of verification.*

Verify System

Select Option

This function performs a range of basic checks on your system to highlight possible Audit or VAT anomalies. The output is a report listing queried items, explaining why each has been identified. You can then decide whether it needs to be corrected.

○ Check Accounts system for potential Audit queries.
   (e.g. possible duplicate transactions)

◉ Run VAT Audit check on Accounts system for possible tax queries.
   (e.g. high VAT - rated transactions)

○ Show all Accounts verification and VAT audit reports.
   (to report on individual areas)

○ Check VAT values on transactions for possible errors.

Please note: This function is only a guide to potential anomalies and it may not be complete. For a definitive assessment on VAT and Audit matters, you should seek advice from your local VAT office.

[Help]   [OK]   [Cancel]

3 *You may need to define this more closely – if you have a lot of transactions, it may be better to look at only one thing at a time.*

VAT Audit Check Settings

| Sales Analysis | Purchase Analysis | Financials Analysis |

Sales Analysis

☑ Identify Sales Invoices and Receipts where tax code is non vatable or not in use.

☐ Identify Sales Invoices and Receipts where:
  - VAT Rate is less than `16.00` % and Tax amount is not equal to zero, and
  - Sales Credits where VAT Rate is more than `19.00` % and Tax amount is not equal to zero.

☐ Identify Sales Credits where:
  - Net Amount equals zero and VAT amount is over `50.00`

☐ Identify EC Sales transactions to Customer accounts with no VAT Registration Number.

☐ Identify EC Sales transactions to non-EU and UK Customers

[Help]   [OK]   [Cancel]

4 *Set the date range and click* **OK.**
5 *Close the window when you have done, or use the tab to switch back to the Financials display.*

9.7 VAT

I like the way VAT is handled – for two reasons. First, Sage 50 does all the work for you! And second, the window follows the design of the standard VAT form, just as the payments screen mimics a cheque, and that makes transferring figures a breeze.

1 *Click* **VAT** *to open the VAT Return window.*

2 *Set the period start and end in the fields at the top right.*
3 *If you want to* **Include Reconciled** *transactions, tick the box.*
4 *Click* **Calculate***. If there are also unreconciled transactions, you will be told and can choose whether to include them.*
5 *If you want a report, click* **Print***.*
6 *Select the* **VAT Return Type** *and the* **Output** *mode.*

VAT Return Report

VAT Return Type
- ☑ VAT return
- ☐ Summary
- ☐ Detailed
- ☐ Adjustment

Output
- ◉ Printer
- ○ Preview
- ○ File
- ○ Email

Run   Cancel

7 *The* **Summary** *report shows the total VAT due on each account;* **Detailed** *shows every transaction that had a VAT component.*
8 *Click* **Run***.*
9 *Calculating VAT has no effect on your data, so you can do it as often as need be – e.g. you may want to run it early to get an idea of the likely amount to pay. Once you have done the final calculation for a period, click* **Reconcile** *to mark the items as processed so that they do not appear in future returns.*
10 *Click* **Close** *when you have done.*

9.8 Managing the month end

The month end routines are optional. Their purpose is to handle recurring entries, update stock and asset valuations and tidy up the customer and supplier accounts, so that you don't have to wade through old data, but to do this without losing essential information. They take time to run, but could save time overall. Look closely at your accounts and talk to your accountant.

There are quite a few steps involved in performing the month end routines, but fortunately Sage 50 gives you a checklist of things to do, and direct links to each operation.

1 *In the* **Financials** *or the* **Company** *module, select* **Manage Month End** *in the* **Tasks** *pane. The* **Period End** *Help display will appear. In the first stage you will be guided through the operations to tidy up the accounts for the month: posting current transactions, dealing with recurring entries, prepayments and accruals, recording depreciation and updating the stock. Some of these may not be relevant to your business or the way you handle your accounts (e.g. do you need to revalue your fixed assets monthly?).*

2 *There are Help pages to guide you through the month end procedures – this is the start of the first stage. At each point there is a direct link to the operation that needs to be done.*

3 *At the second stage, you will be prompted to make a backup so have your backup media ready. After setting the program date to the month end date, the month end procedure is run.*

4 *The* **Month End...** *dialog box has four options – check those which are relevant and click* **OK**.

5   *Setting Month End options. Note these two: Clear Turnover Figures resets customer and Supplier monthly turnover figures to zero. Post Depreciation will calculate depreciation for you if fixed assets have been recorded in the Fixed Assets register.*

6   *At the third stage you will be prompted to create a second backup. The remaining steps are optional. You can clear your stock activity and/or the audit trail. And if you do either or both of these, you will need to take another backup afterwards. Let's have a closer look at clearing the audit trail.*

CLEARING THE AUDIT TRAIL

Clearing removes all those transactions that have been fully paid, reconciled with the bank statement and processed for the VAT return. Before they are erased, the routine calculates the effect of the transactions on the accounts and rewrites the opening balances.

How long you keep transactions in the Audit Trail is for you and your accountant to decide. The Sage 50 system is capable of storing up to 2 billion transactions so space is not an issue (as long as your hard disk is big enough and your backup media can cope with the file sizes). Speed – or rather the lack of it – may become an issue, as response time can slow down with very large files. Normal practice is for the Audit Trail to be cleared as part of your regular end-of-period routines.

To clear the audit trail:

1   *You must have hard copies of all your transactions before you clear the trail. Print the reports for the Audit Trail, Monthly Day Books, Sales, Purchase and Nominal Activity and VAT Return.*

2   *If you have not done so already, back up your data.*

3   *Start the Clear Audit Trail wizard from the final stage of the Month End routine, or open the* **Tools** *menu, point to* **Period End** *and select* **Clear Audit Trail**.

4 Read the prompts and warnings as you work through the wizard. At the third stage, enter the date to clear up to – this will typically be the last month end.

Clear Audit Trail Wizard

Clear Audit Trail

Confirming your Clear Audit Trail date

The clear audit trail process will remove fully paid and reconciled transactions from the audit trail up to a specified date.

Enter the date you want to remove transactions up to: `31/07/2009`

* Note - To enable accurate credit control reporting you should keep at least three months live data.

Important!

It is essential that you take a backup of your data before clearing the audit trail. If you do not have a backup of your data, please select the Backup Now option to take a copy of your data.

Make a backup copy of my data `Backup Now` * Note - Not available in Demo Mode

Click Next to continue.

[Cancel] [Help]   [Back] [Next] [Finish]

---

5 When the wizard has done its work, you will be offered a chance to view the transactions that have been cleared. View them, and print the report for your records. You cannot be too careful with your data.

9.9 The Year End routine

The Year End procedure is a little simpler than that of the Month End – its main purpose is to transfer summary figures to the Prior Year – and it must be preceded by the Month End routine for month 12, where the bulk of the work is done.

Backups and printouts to secure old data are key parts of this procedure, so have your backup media and paper ready!

1 *Select* **Manage Year End** *in the Tasks. The* **Period End** *Help display will appear. Work through it, clicking the icons as needed to go back into the system to run backups, printing and other operations.*

2 *In Step 3, run the Year End option.*

3 At the **Year End** *dialog box, select the* **Output** *mode – Printer or File.*
4 *If you use the budgeting facilities, tick the checkboxes to transfer the actual figures to the budgets, and to generate next year's budgets (setting increases if appropriate).*
5 *Double check that you have all the necessary backups and printouts, and if you have, click* **OK** *to run the routine.*
6 *The final stages of the Year End procedure are about tidying up – clearing old data and removing accounts which are no longer in use.*

THINGS TO REMEMBER

▶ *The Audit Trail is the full record of all transactions that are still awaiting further processing. It should be cleared as part of the end-of-period routines to remove fully reconciled transactions.*

▶ *The Trial Balance provides a summary of the state of the accounts – and if it doesn't balance, worry! If there are values in Suspense or Mispostings, investigate!*

▶ *The Profit and Loss account and Balance Sheet are based on a selected Chart of Accounts.*

▶ *Sage 50 will calculate the figures for the VAT return and display them in the same layout as the VAT form. Before running the VAT routine you should verify your data.*

▶ *The Month End and Year End routines tidy up the system and calculate new end-of-period totals.*

10

Products

In this chapter you will learn:
- *how to create product records*
- *how to view and edit product records*
- *about price lists and pricing structures*
- *how to record stock movements*

10.1 The Products module

The Products module is one of the less interactive parts of the
system – which figures, as there is not a lot you can do with the
products, except keep a track of them and use product information
in the creation of invoices. The tools in this window let you create
new product records, edit existing records, update stock levels,
maintain price lists and print the information.

If you have a large inventory, maintaining full, accurate product
and price lists can be quite time-consuming, but it delivers faster,
more efficient invoicing and should save much more time in the
long run.

Product defaults

Before you do any work on your products, check and set the
defaults – see page 75.

10.2 New products

New product records are set up through a wizard. This will ask
for a range of details, not all of which may be relevant to your
business. Don't waste time entering useless information. If any
details are not known when you are working on the wizard, leave
them and enter them later by editing the product record.

▶ *The* Description, Code, Sale Price, Tax Code, Unit of Sale *and*
Nominal Code *are essential.*
▶ Location, Commodity Code, Weight, Purchase A/C *code and*
(supplier's) Part No. *can be often omitted.*

1 *In the* Product *window, click* New.
2 *Click* Next *to get past the first page and enter a* Description.
The Code *will be created from this – edit it if necessary.*

3 *Enter the* Location, Category *and other details if wanted.*

4 *Enter the* **Sale Price,** *and change the* **Sales Nominal Code, Unit of Sale, Tax Code** *and* **Department** *if the defaults do not suit.*

5 *Select the* **Supplier A/C** *and enter the* **Part No., Re-Order Level** *and* **Quantity** *and* **Cost Price** *if wanted.*

Product Record Wizard

Product Information

Entering your product purchase details.

Enter the purchase details of this new product record, i.e. Supplier account and Supplier part no.

Supplier A/C	SUP001	Re-Order Level	100.00
Part No.	LEXVE4G	Re-Order Qty	25.00
Purchase Nominal Code	5000	Cost Price	4.30

Cancel   Help   Back   Next   Finish

6 *You will be asked if you want to set an opening balance. If you do, select* **Yes** *then enter the* **Reference, Date, Quantity** *and* **Cost Price** *– this is the price per unit, not the total.*

Product Record Wizard

Product Information

Choosing to enter your products opening balance

Do you wish to post an opening balance for your new product?

- ○ No, there is no opening balance to enter.
- ⦿ Yes, I wish to enter an opening balance.

Cancel   Help   Back   Next   Finish

7 *Click* **Finish** *to save the product data.*

10.3 Viewing and editing product data

The product records contain the information that you entered
when you first created it, plus details of any sales or other stock
movements. There is also a Memo tab for any notes you want to
add, a BOM (bill of materials) tab, where the components of a
compound product can be listed, and a Web tab which can hold
images and text for use in web pages.

If prices or other details have changed, or if there are errors or
omissions in your product data, the records are easily edited.

1 *Select the record(s) you want to edit.*
2 *Click* **Record.**
3 *Edit the record. Add details to the* **Memo** *tab if required.*

4 *If the product is made up from separate components – each with their own product record – switch to the* **BOM** *tab. Select each component in the* **Product Code** *field, and set the* **Quantity** *value – Sage 50 will fill the remaining fields.*

5 *Click* Save.

6 *Click* **Next** *if there are more records, or select a new record from the* **Product Code** *at the top left and repeat steps 3 to 5.*

7 *Click* **Close.**

Creating Product records while invoicing

If, while generating an invoice, you find that a product is not on the system, click the New button on the Products list.

A Product Record window will open to collect essential details.

10.4 Price lists

If you sell products at different prices according to the nature of the customer – as opposed to, or as well as, giving discounts to categories of customers – these can be handled by Sage 50.

A price list has two aspects: the products and their prices, and the customers to whom those prices apply. If price lists exist, when you add a product to an invoice, Sage 50 will check the lists to see which price to use for the customer. If the customer is not on any list, the standard price will be applied.

To create a price list:

1 *Click the* **Prices** *button on the toolbar.*

2 *At the* **Price Lists** *window, click* **New.**

Name	Description	Type	Last Updated	Currency
TRADEA	Trade Price List A	Customer		Pound Sterling
TRADEB	Trade Price List B	Customer		Pound Sterling

New Edit Delete Print Copy Close

3 *You will be asked which type of price list you wish to create.
Click* **Customer.** *(Supplier lists are a bit different, but simpler.)*

4 *At the* **New Price List** *window, enter a* **Name** *and a*
Description *for the list. Click* **Add** *to add the first product to
the list. (The window will change its title to* **Edit Price List.**)

5 *At the* **Add Products** *dialog box, select an item from the list.*

6 *You can set a fixed price, or decrease or increase the cost price or the current sale price by a percentage or a value. As percentage changes can produce fractional amounts, these can be rounded up or down. You can also work in multiples with an adjustment, e.g. whole pounds minus 1p to give 3.99, 6.99 prices.*

7 *Click* **OK** *to add the product and its price to the list.*

8 *Click* **Save** *and repeat steps 5 to 7 for the other products.*

You can add selected customers to a list so that its prices are applied when they place an order. This is going to be of most use with lists for trade customers.

9 *Switch to the* **Customers** *tab.*

10 *Click* **Add.**

Add Customers [RETAIL1 - Over the counter sales to public]

Choose customers from the list:

A/C	Name	Price List
A1D001	A1 Design Services	... TRADE
ABS001	ABS Garages Ltd	... TRADE
BBS001	Bobs Building Supplies	... TRADE
BRI001	Fred Briant	...
BRO001	Bronson Inc	... TRADE
BUS001	Business Exhibitions	...
CASH001	Cash and Credit Card Sal...	
CGS001	County Golf Supplies	... TRADE
COM001	Compton Packaging	... TRADE
DATARECO	Data Recovery Ltd	...
DST001	Johnson Design & Bu...	TRADE
FGL001	F G Landscape & Design	...
GRA001	Graham Electonics	...

OK   Cancel

11 *Select a customer to whom the price will apply. Click* **OK**.
12 *Repeat* 10 *and* 11 *to add all the relevant customers.*
13 *If you later want to remove a customer from a list, select the name and click* **Remove**.
14 *Click* **Save** *and* **Close**.

Pricing Structures

The Pricing Structure button on the Details tab of the product record opens a window from where you can add a new price list, or create a special price for a single customer. The latter process is much the same as making a price list for a product.

10.5 Stock levels

The Product records can be used to keep track of stock levels. You can enter the quantities in stock when first setting up a record or after a stocktake. If goods are sold via invoices, the movements out are automatically marked on the product record when the invoice is posted. Deliveries, non-invoiced sales and other movements are handled through the In and Out routines in the Product module.

STOCK MOVEMENTS

The Products module has three routines for recording changes:

▶ *In (adjustment in) – deliveries and returns.*
▶ *Out (adjustment out) – sales and losses.*
▶ *Stock Take – updating the files after a manual stocktake.*

The In and Out dialog boxes are identical except that the In box also has a field to record the current cost, and in the Out dialog box this is replaced by one showing the current stock levels.

Transfers

There is a stock transfer facility to handle products assembled from several components.

To record movement:

1 *Select the products to be adjusted. This is not essential as products can be selected at step 3, but it may be simpler to select them all at the start.*
2 *Click* **In** *or* **Out.**

Product Code	Details	Date	Ref.	Project Ref	Cost Code	Quantity	Cost Price	Sale Price	On order	Free
MEM001	DIMM 32mb 100Mhz	30/12/2008				50.00	22.00	30.00	0.00	63.00
MEM002	DIMM 64mb 100Mhz	30/12/2008				50.00	43.00	58.00	0.00	59.00
MEM003	DIMM 128mb 100M...	30/12/2008				25.00		100.00	0.00	34.00

Stock Adjustments In

Save   Discard   Print List   Close

3 *Select the* **Product Code,** *if necessary.*

4 The **Date** *will be set to the program date. Adjust if necessary.*
5 *Enter a* **Ref** *and/or* **Project Ref** *if required.*
6 *Enter the* **Quantity**.
7 *With In movements,* change the **Cost Price** *if it is different from the default.*
8 *Repeat steps 3 to 7 for other products.*
9 *Click* **Save**.
10 *Click* **Close**.

To run a stocktake:
1 *Select the products, or leave this until step 3.*
2 *Click the* **Stock Take** *button.*

Product Code	Details	Date	Ref	Actual	Cost Price	In stock	Adjustment
MOTH001	MTH1000 Motherbo...	30/12/2008	STK TAKE	8.00	30.00	9.00	-1.00
MOTH002	MTH2000 Motherbo...	30/12/2008	STK TAKE	8.00	40.00	8.00	0.00
MOTH003	MTH3000 Motherbo...	30/12/2008	STK TAKE	13.00	50.00	13.00	0.00

Save   Discard   Memorise   Recall   Print List   Close

3 *Select the* **Product Code,** *if necessary.*
4 *Adjust the* **Date** *if necessary.*
5 *Enter the* **Actual** *number in stock.*
6 *Repeat steps 3 to 5 for other products.*
7 *Click* **Save** *then* **Close**.

THINGS TO REMEMBER

▶ *Product records are produced through the Product Record Wizard. Non-essential information can be omitted or added later.*

▶ *In the Products module you can create new product records, edit old records, update stock levels and print details of your products.*

▶ *Details can be edited at any time, simply select the records and click the Record button to start.*

▶ *Price lists allow you to maintain different pricing structures for different categories of customer.*

▶ *Stock levels are updated as goods are sold through invoices, and can also be adjusted through the In, Out and Stock Take routines.*

11

··

Help and support

In this chapter you will learn:
- *about browsing the Help system*
- *how to locate Help through the index or a search*
- *about advice and support from Sage on the Web*
- *about the shortcut keys*

11.1 Help

Sage 50 systems have very many features. Some of these you may never use, as they are not applicable to your business, others will be used only rarely, at year-ends or when particular problems arise. So, though you will soon be at ease with the routine chores – most of which should be covered in this book – there will be times when you find yourself saying, 'How do I do this?' At times like this, turn first to the Help pages. To find information, you can browse through the **Contents**, look it up in the **Index** or **Search** for it.

If the Help pages alone do not provide the answer, there is more information, technical support and other types of Help available online at Sage's website.

11.2 Contents

The Contents panel offers the best approach when you are looking for Help with a module or operation. Here, the Help pages are organized into sections, with two or three levels of subdivisions. If the first page that you find does not tell you quite what you want to know, look for the links to related pages, and follow these up to find the answer.

▶ *Look in the* Welcome *and* Setting up *sections for Help with the use of the software.*
▶ *Look in the* Accounts *and* Bookkeeping Information *section for Help with accounting concepts and techniques.*
▶ *Look in the* Glossary *for explanations of accounting or computing terms.*

1 *Open the* **Help** *menu and click* **Contents and Index**.

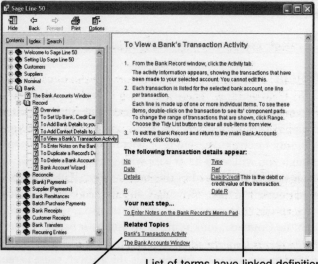

List of terms have linked definitions

Many pages have links to related topics

2 *If necessary, click the* **Contents** *tab.*
3 *Click* ⊞ *to open a section. Most have subsections – click a second level* ⊞ *to reach the pages.*
4 *Click* 📄 *to display a page in the main pane.*
5 *If the display is getting crowded, click* ⊟ *to close up unwanted branches.*

NAVIGATING A HELP PAGE

At the top of any page in the Help system, you will find five icons:

▶ 🔙 *Back takes you back to the last page you were looking at*

▶ 🔘 *Questions takes you to the Frequently Asked Questions page for the topic, where you will find answers to many of your queries*

▶ 📖 *Book takes you to the 'Book' page for the topic, which holds a set of links to related topics*

▶ 📑 *Show shows all the drop-down text (see below) on the page, then changes to become...* 📑 *Hide which closes up all drop-down text*

▶ 🖨 *Print sends the current page to the printer.*

The Back and Print commands are repeated in the tools at the top left of the Help window. There are two others there: Hide, which we will come back to in 11.5, and Forward which becomes active after you have used Back and takes you on again to where you were before.

Every page contains links of one sort or another. Linked text comes in two varieties. It is always in cyan – as are headings, but they are in a bigger, bold font.

▶ *If the text is underlined, then clicking on it will take you to a linked page.*
▶ *If it is not underlined, clicking on it will drop-down an explanation of the term – click again to hide it.*

The **Help** window sits on top of the other Sage 50 windows. When you have done, close it or minimize it out of the way if you want to refer to it again later.

11.3 The Help Index

The Index contains nearly 2500 entries and sub-entries, in alphabetical order. You can scroll through to find an entry, but it is quicker to type in the first few letters of a word and jump to the relevant part of the Index.

Most entries lead to a single page, but sometimes you will be offered a choice of pages from the same word.

If you were using the Index when you last shut down Help, the **Contents and Index** option will reopen Help at the Index.

1 *Open the* **Help** *menu and select* **Contents and Index**.
2 *If necessary, click the* **Index** *tab*.
3 *Drag the slider to scroll through the Index*.
or
4 *Type the first few letters of the word to jump to the right part of the list*.
5 *Double-click on an entry or select it and click* **Display**.
6 *If the* **Topics Found** *panel opens to offer you a choice – select one and click* **Display**.

11.4 Searching for Help

A Search hunts through the entire text of the Help system. It normally produces more results, as it will find every page containing a given word – not just the main ones on the topic. This can be useful as you can get a more thorough understanding of an issue by following up all the leads, but if all you want to do is find the meaning of a word, or learn how to do a particular job, it can take a bit longer to locate the relevant page.

If you were using the Search when you last shut down Help, the **Contents and Index** option reopens Help at the **Search** panel.

1 *Open the* **Help** *menu or click the* **Help** *button and select* **Contents and Index**.
2 *If necessary, click the* **Search** *tab.*
3 *Type one or more words to define the Help you need.*
4 *Click* **List Topics**.
5 *Select a topic from the bottom pane.*
6 *Click* **Display**.

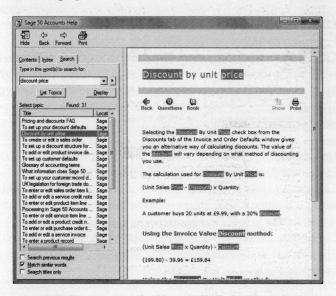

11.5 The navigation panel

If you want to work on your accounts while keeping the Help window open, you may need to adjust your screen display so that you can see what you are doing.

Like any other window, the Help window can be resized and moved, but the most effective way to reduce its size is to hide the navigation panel. You can still go back through recently opened pages, or follow links from the current page, and if you need to get back into it, to find a different Help page, it is easily opened again.

1 *Click* ▣ *to close the navigation panel.*
2 *Work through your task, using the Help page for guidance as needed.*
3 *Click* ▣ *if you need to open the navigation panel again.*

11.6 Sage on the Web

The options on the WebLinks menu connect you to the Internet and take you to Sage's website. Browsing through the site, you will find mainly news and information about Sage's products and services, along with some good articles on major topics. If you are looking for in-depth answers to more complex questions, then you should head to the Ask Sage area, but to get there, you need to subscribe to SageCover.

SageCover

SageCover gives you access, via e-mail or phone, to additional expert advice and assistance with Sage systems and with accountancy and other aspects of business in general. It is free for the first six weeks after purchasing Sage software. Continuing cover can be bought online from the Sage shop. The cost varies depending upon the software, the number of users and the level of support required.

Registration and logging in

Before you can get into the SageCover members' areas, you need to register with Sage. For this you will need your account number or the serial number of your software. Dig out the box! It's in there. Once you have registered, you can log in and use the members' areas.

11.7 Ask Sage

Ask Sage is a database of thousands of articles across a wide range of business and accounting activities. Use this to quickly locate the information that you need – just enter one or more keywords to focus the search.

▶ *If you can't find an answer in the Knowledgebase, go to* **Ask Support** *and e-mail your problem to their support staff.*

1 *Open the* **Weblinks** *menu and select* **SageCover Ask Sage.**
2 *If you are looking for information from the customer service side of Sage, then select a Product and a subsection, otherwise leave this blank.*

3 *In the Keywords box, type some words to define what you are looking for.*

4 *Click* **Search.**

5 *Click on an article's title to read it. It will open in a new window.*

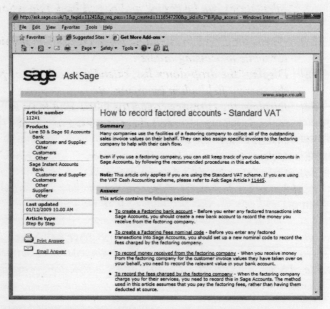

There are over 10,000 articles in the ask sage database! asking very specific questions can help to locate the right information, but sometimes it is better to use only a single keyword and then browse the results. you will see that some are 'step by step' to walk you through a process, and others are classed as 'definitions and summaries'.

11.8 Shortcut keys

When the Sage system is active, the function keys [F1] to [F12] all have special purposes.

Check these out after you have been using the Sage system for a little while and see which ones it would be useful to learn. Though all functions can be accessed easily through the menus or toolbar buttons, when you are typing it is handy to be able to get to them directly from the keyboard.

You might like to note these in particular:

- ▶ *[F1]* *Displays the Help system.*
- ▶ *[F2]* *Runs Windows calculator – the results of the calculations can be copied and pasted back into a Sage 50 field.*
- ▶ *[F3]* *Opens the Edit Line window when creating an invoice (or while processing orders).*
- ▶ *[F4]* *Displays the drop-down list, calendar or calculator from the current field when invoicing, etc.*
- ▶ *[F5]* *Displays the currency convertor when used from a numeric field or the spell checker from a text field.*
- ▶ *[F7]* *Inserts a line into an invoice.*
- ▶ *[F8]* *Deletes the current line of an invoice.*
- ▶ *[F9]* *Calculates the VAT from a net price.*
- ▶ *[F12]* *Launches Report Designer.*

THINGS TO REMEMBER

▶ *There is plenty of Help available. You can browse through the Contents, or search for information in the Index or Search panels.*

▶ *If you want to refer to the Help window while working in the Sage window, you can hide its navigation panel so it takes up less space.*

▶ *You can start your Internet browser from within Sage 50. Any browser can be used, though Internet Explorer is recommended by Sage and is best for interactive support.*

▶ *The Sage website has some useful information on its public pages and a great deal more in its SageCover section.*

▶ *The Knowledgebase is a valuable source of help on many aspects of Sage software and accountancy.*

▶ *The function keys have shortcuts to some common operations.*

Index